Inquiry-based Teaching With PBL

34 Projects

by Jacqui Murray and Ask a Tech Teacher

2023
V1.2

Part of the Structured Learning Technology for the Classroom series

ALL MATERIAL IN THIS BOOK IS PROTECTED BY THE INTELLECTUAL PROPERTY LAWS OF THE USA.

No part of this work can be reproduced or used in any form or by any means—graphic, electronic, or mechanical, including photocopying, recording, taping, Web distribution or information storage and retrieval systems—without the prior written permission of the publisher

For permission to use material from this text or product, contact us by email at:
info@structuredlearning.net

ISBN 978-1-942101-51-2

Printed in the United States of America

Introduction

Today's classroom is all about authentic lessons that are inquiry-driven, student-centered, with technology that is critical but invisible—just another part of the lesson. The new educational mandates require students share, show evidence of learning, collaborate on outcomes, and publish their work.

The question we get often from teachers—both new and seasoned—is: *How do you teach technology skills (i.e., the use of foundational programs like word processing and keyboarding) in an inquiry-based classroom?*

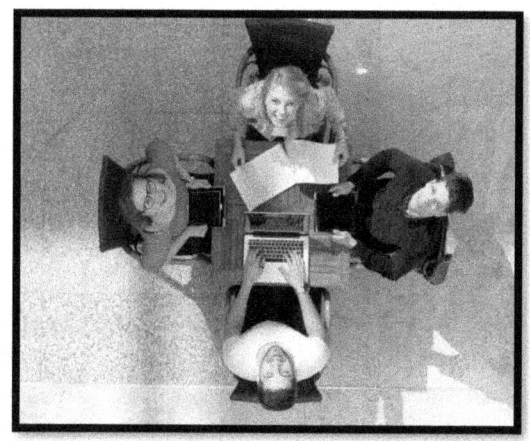

Inquiry-based teaching requires a mindset that makes curiosity a cornerstone of learning, that organizes a classroom to encourage that, and forms lessons that value and ultimately assess it. Before we get into how this book accomplishes that, let's discuss:

The Inquiry-based Teacher

The Inquiry-based Classroom

The Socratic Method

Project-based Learning (PBL)

The next four sections detail what an inquiry-based teacher is, how s/he can set up an inquiry-based classroom, and how to implement this using either the Socratic Method and/or project-based learning.

The Inquiry-based Teacher

Inquiry is considered an effective education strategy that develops passionate, life-long learners. It sounds simple enough--ask questions and observe answers—but it's much more. You listen with all your senses, respond to what you heard (not what you wanted to hear), keep your eye on the class Big Ideas, value everyone's contribution, and plug into the class's energy. You step in when needed and step aside when required. You aren't a teacher, rather a guide. You and the class find your way from question to knowledge together.

Because everyone learns differently.

Inquiry-based Teaching with PBL

You use a textbook as a map to show how to get from here to there, not as a to-do list.

In an inquiry-based classroom, you know where you're going but not quite how to get there and that's a good thing. You are no longer that teacher who stood in front of rows of students and pointed to the blackboard. You operate well outside your comfort zone as you try out the flipped classroom, student-led conferences, gamified learning, SEL, peer feedback, and more--and are thrilled with the results.

And then there's the issue of assessment. What your students accomplish can't neatly be summed up by a multiple choice test. When you review what you thought would assess learning (back when you designed the lesson), none measure the organic conversations the class had, the risk-taking they engaged in to arrive at answers, knowledge transfer that popped up independent of class time. You realize you must open your mind to learning that you never taught--never saw coming in the weeks you stood amongst your students guiding their education.

Let me digress. I visited the Soviet Union (back when it was one nation) and dropped in on a classroom where students were inculcated with how things must be done. It was a polite, respectful, ordered experience but lacked cerebral energy, without the joy of learning and the wow factor as students independently figured out how to do something. When that nation ended, I arrived at different conclusions than the politicians and the economists. I saw a nation starved for creativity. Without creativity, learning didn't transfer. Without transfer, it collapsed in on itself like a hollowed out orange.

So how do you become an inquiry-based teacher? Here's advice from fellow teachers:

1. *ask open-ended questions and be open-minded about conclusions*
2. *provide hands-on experiences*
3. *use groups to foster learning*
4. *encourage self-paced learning*
5. *be open to the student who learns less but deeper as well as the student who learns a wider breadth*
6. *differentiate instruction*
7. *look for evidence of learning in unusual places. It may be from the child with his/her hand up or the learner who teaches mom how to use email.*
8. *understand assessment comes in many shapes--a summative quiz, a formative simulation, a rubric, or a game that requires knowledge to succeed. It may be anecdotal or peer-to-peer. Whatever approach shows students are transferring knowledge from your class to life is legitimate.*

9. *be flexible. Class won't always (probably never) go as your mind's eye saw it. That's OK. Learn with students. Observe their progress and adapt to their path.*
10. *give up the idea that teaching requires control. Refer to #8--Be flexible*
11. *facilitate student learning in a way that works for them. Trust they will come up with the questions required to reach the Big Ideas.*

In the end, know that inquiry-based teaching creates life-long learners. These are the individuals who will solve the world's future problems.

The Inquiry-based Classroom

Let's say you consider yourself an inquiry-based teacher. The next step is to make your classroom fit that model. Until the inquiry-based classroom became popular, the goal of teaching seemed to be to follow a well-trod path rather than to achieve an important goal. When the concept of the inquiry-based classroom arrived, you came alive. This was what you'd hoped to do when you started teaching. But how do you turn a traditional entrenched classroom into one that's inquiry-based?

You do it one step at a time. Here are fifteen.

Remember: Inquiry is about curiosity and exploration, not about following a to-do list. Pick which e work for you. With these, morph your classroom from passive to sparkling, from boring to brilliant.

Flip the classroom

The flipped classroom inverts traditional teaching methods by delivering instruction outside of class (probably online) and moving what is traditionally considered 'homework' into the classroom.

The night prior to coming to class, students read the lecture materials so you can spend class time in hands-on discovery.

Don't answer student questions--show them how to do it themselves

When students have questions, guide them toward answers. Don't give them a fish. Teach them to fish. When students understand the methodology, they can repeat the process. Without that, they are robots.

But doesn't this require comprehensive teacher preparation to be ready for the multitude of directions a conversation can go? Well, not really if you understand your subject. But you may pull pieces from many parts of your curriculum. Rather than steer student inquiry within the confines of a pre-defined lesson, students let their curiosity go where it will.

Inquiry-based lessons are process-, not product-oriented. How students reach conclusions is as important as the conclusions they reach. That critical thinking is what it's about. Think back to your favorite school lessons. Were they learning the capital of every state or completing a project by following the scientific method? (OK, maybe that doesn't work but you get my point--your favorite lessons required you to think, not regurgitate).

Listen when students speak

It's tempting to think you know what students are going to ask/say. Resist the impulse. Listen to them. Try to understand what their real question is, not what their words say. Watch them. Are they comfortable with your answer or do they squirm? Take the time to travel the distance to a solution.

Encourage questions.

Class is ticking away and there are too many questions. If you take time to answer all of them, you won't cover the scheduled material.

That's OK. Take the time. An odd thing will start to happen. As students more thoroughly understand a concept, they will transfer that knowledge to other lessons and those will go faster than expected. By the end of the year, you'll have covered more material in more depth. Cool, hunh?

Spend time on projects, not lecturing

There's an old Chinese proverb, although Ben Franklin occasionally gets credit for these words:

"Tell me and I'll forget.

Show me and I may remember.

Involve me and I'll understand."

Inquiry is about doing, not observing, action not inaction.

Lessons are fluid

Learning isn't linear. It's a web that grows out from the guiding question. As such, your lesson plan may change dramatically based on student inquiry. If you teach three fifth-grade classes, each will likely be different from the other. That's OK. Your challenge is to track what you did in each class and pick up from where you left off. That's OK, too. It's part of teaching an inquiry-based class.

Publish and share

Inquiry-based classrooms share knowledge. This can be accomplished via a class wiki, blog, website, discussion board, Facebook page, or Twitter feed--but it's done. Students understand how to embed articles and projects to be shared with everyone. Students accept that part of their responsibility is to ask questions about shared materials, read and comment on them, and use them as resources. We all grow when one grows.

Reflection is included in every lesson plan

What did students learn? Where can they transfer it? You as teacher do that after every teaching experience. Your students must do it also. Then you understand if what they learned was what you planned. Or something else.

You are a fellow learner

Students are valued. Their conclusions bend discussion, mold learning. In this way, they understand the importance of their participation in projects, reflections, and collaborative experiences. Encourage this. Accept that the inquiry-based classroom will be noisier than the typical class--and that's a good thing.

Questions don't have yes-no answers

They are open-ended, more about 'how' and 'why', which requires investigation into multiple strands to answer well. Assessment, then, becomes the student ability to use problem-solving and thinking skills, not to repeat someone else's conclusions.

Summative assessments are hands-on, creative, and student-centered

They are less about answering teacher questions than sharing student learning. You might even have students create their own assessments in something like PuzzleMaker.

If you use the Socrative Method in your class, this will feel familiar.

The Socratic Method

Have you ever walked into a classroom where students were engaged in serious on-topic discussion, debating ideas and challenging each other to provide evidence of their statements? And when you looked around for the teacher, s/he was calmly sitting in the back, observing, taking it all in but not participating?

Chances are, you entered a classroom using a discussion method known as **Socratic Debate**, aka **Socratic Method, Socratic Circle**, or **Socratic Inquiry**. Many teachers try this approach when they realize lecturing doesn't engage students anymore. Sure, class members can memorize facts but too often the critical thinking required to analyze cause and effect — say, how a specific river encouraged ancient trade — eludes them unless the teacher spells it out, telling them the "right" answer.

In a traditional classroom, asking and answering questions is stressful to many students who are afraid their answer will be wrong. This is where the student-directed, no-right-wrong-answer Socratic Method shines.

It all started with this (supposed) quote from the iconic Greek thinker, Socrates:

> *"Let us examine the question together, my friend, and if you can contradict anything I say, do so and I will be persuaded."*

This ancient form of give-and-take discourse is reportedly founded on Socrates' belief that lecture was not an effective way to teach all students. The **Socratic Method** requires cooperative argumentative dialogue between individuals, asking and answering questions that stimulate critical thinking and draw out underlying presumptions. Students prepare by closely reading and researching the text or topic. On the day of the Socratic Seminar, they listen to classmates, challenge what they hear by building an argument based on what they have read and heard, and in so doing critically think about not

only their opinions but those of classmates. This encourages listening, thinking, reading, speaking critically, and feeling a sense of wonder about the world's knowledge. Students quickly figure out that to succeed in the Socratic Method, they must arrive prepared to share and listen and reflect.

Through this process, with subtle guidance from the instructor, students learn to teach themselves. Their goal is to analyze facts, not find the perfect answer. The Socratic Method is not passive. Students don't consume; they create, participate, and gain a deeper understanding of the topic. The goal has nothing to do with who wins the argument but how evidence and ideas are presented.

How to use it in your Classroom

- Remind students to arrive having prepared the required material.
- Set the stage for this questioning approach by discussing the power of questions in resolving issues.
- Arrange students in two comfortable circles, the inner circle for talking and the outer for listening. These should be set up so students can see each other and interact easily. If the group is small, you may have just one circle.
- All students (and you) must know each other's names, even at the first meeting.
- Set down conversation guidelines like 1) refer to each other by name, 2) participate by building on conversations, 3) participate often with comments and reactions to ideas of others, 4) don't dominate the stage, 5) disagree but don't be disagreeable, and 6) wait your turn.
- Remind students there are no right or wrong answers.
- Remind students to focus on concepts and principles, not first person narratives. Personal experiences are fine, but they must be woven into the context of the conversation.
- As the teacher, you won't be either the "sage on the stage" or "guide on the side". You are part of a learning group. You pose well-structured, open-ended questions and then expect students to lead the discussion. Ideally, questions are not a stopping point but a beginning to further analysis and research.
- Keep the conversation on track — don't let it veer in an entirely new direction without finding how that connects to earlier comments.
- Be comfortable with the silence. Students need time to think.
- Be comfortable learning from students. It's not always clear where questions will end up.

Why it's popular

One of the biggest reasons for the Socratic Method's popularity is that it encourages and rewards higher-order thinking skills like evaluating, analyzing, and applying. These mindsets help students learn independently and develop them into life-long learners.

But it's not only about sharing ideas. It's about honing listening skills — deep listening. Students begin to love learning because it comes from themselves and peers. Students develop an understanding of the difference between arguing and discussing: The former is emotional; the latter while still impassioned, is respectful.

For Common Core schools, the Socratic Method prods students to:

- *use text-based evidence to support ideas*
- *identify/evaluate claims and counterclaims*
- *summarize points of agreement*
- *prepare for a discussion*
- *practice drawing inferences from texts*
- *initiate and participate effectively in discussions*
- *pose and respond to questions that relate to the discussion*
- *practice using conventions and domain-specific vocabulary when speaking*
- *gain understanding of other perspectives*

What are its drawbacks

The Socratic Method wants teachers and students to follow a conversation where it goes. If the discussion goes afield, so it does. The Socratic Method is well-suited to conversations such as "if a tree falls in the forest, does it make a noise". As a result, and with a nod toward the constraints of curriculum and lesson plan goals, many teachers provide guidance in reaching the day's Big Idea.

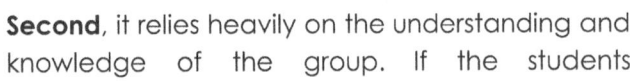

Second, it relies heavily on the understanding and knowledge of the group. If the students misunderstand a concept, the conversation has little chance to arrive at the truth.

Third, this approach works particularly well when students are learning about ethics, the philosophy behind an event, or the morals of a situation. Students must dig into their background to determine the motivations and assumptions behind their beliefs and then use that evidence to defend their thoughts. If/when that becomes impossible, likely the student adapts to a new reality.

Fourth, this approach is not quick. It relies on interaction between individuals, analyzing evidence, questioning everything, and being ready to change ideas.

Finally, this approach is not well-suited to webinars, a flipped classroom, or any other teaching method where students view resources without the opportunity to question them.

Though questioning beliefs can be a painful process, the Socratic Method includes two tools that make it effective: **an open mind** and **respect for those around you**. To provide this sort of gathering to students is a gift, arguably rarely seen since the amphitheaters of ancient Greece.

— image credit: Fresno Public Schools
—image credit: Wong, H.K., Wong, R.T. (2009) *The First Days of School*. Mountain View, CA

Project-based Learning (PBL)

The final piece of inquiry-based teaching—and maybe the most critical—is adaptable lesson plans that rely on Project-based Learning—PBL.

What is PBL?

Project-based learning (PBL) asks teachers to act as facilitators, not lecturers, guiding students to find the necessary answers for the theme-related project. Students are no longer passive listeners who expect the teacher to have all the answers. In fact, students take charge of their own learning as they make choices about how to learn, plan how it should be done, solve their own problems, and present the results to fellow learners.

How does it work?

No matter the project, it must include clearly identifiable goals to be achieved and a roadmap of how students will accomplish them. The teacher starts with an introduction to the subject, including what students can expect to learn, but lecturing ends there. Students are then broken into groups (or not; PBL can be done as individuals also) and they decide what type of project would best address the goals required by the teacher in the opening monologue. A good example of PBL is Genius Hour where students use their passion for a subject to learn more, hone research skills, engage in problem-solving, and then present their findings to classmates in hopes of inciting their interest. As students work, they learn to rely on themselves or their group. Teachers spend their time monitoring student progress and providing guidance to keep students on-target.

At first glance, a PBL class may seem chaotic as students engage in a myriad of approaches to completing projects that address goals -- but real learning is messy. Have faith that **from chaos comes learning** and the joy of unraveling complicated problems students thought they couldn't. Don't worry if as the teacher, you seem unhelpful or even wrong in your answers (especially if their topic is something they've researched in more depth than your knowledge). That's part of learning-by-doing.

Finish the project with class presentations. In this way, students organize their ideas and give classmates the opportunity to learn along with them. Encourage the audience to ask questions and the presenter to elaborate on a theme and provide evidence for their thoughts.

Why teachers like PBL

Here are reasons why more and more teachers I talk to turn to PBL to excite learning among students:

- The essential components of PBL are critical thinking, collaboration, and communication. These align well with the environment students are most likely to be part of after graduation.
- Students who actively create a project to support learning absorb the knowledge more deeply and remember it longer.
- PBL adapts well to differentiated needs because students come up with the project to guide them in learning. Students can use videos, audio recordings, news articles, art, plays, or any other material that works best for their learning and communication style.
- Students are engaged as they mastermind the solution to problems and the answers to questions. This instinctively is what humans like to do.
- As students learn how to answer questions and solve problems on their own, they develop a skill that is transferable to many other parts of life.

How to Use This Book

In this book, you find diverse and varied inquiry-based lesson plans, broken down by grade. All are project-based and flexible. They're easy to understand, fascinating to students, and quickly accomplish what might seem to be the impossible goals of integrating and sharing.

If you find webtools you aren't familiar with, search for them on your browser. Most pop up quickly. If not, visit the Ask a Tech Teacher website resources. The focus is on easy-to-use online tools (with some exceptions) that are quick to teach, inquiry-driven, intuitive, and free. You introduce the tool, demonstrate the project, answer clarifying questions, and let students loose.

Each lesson includes:

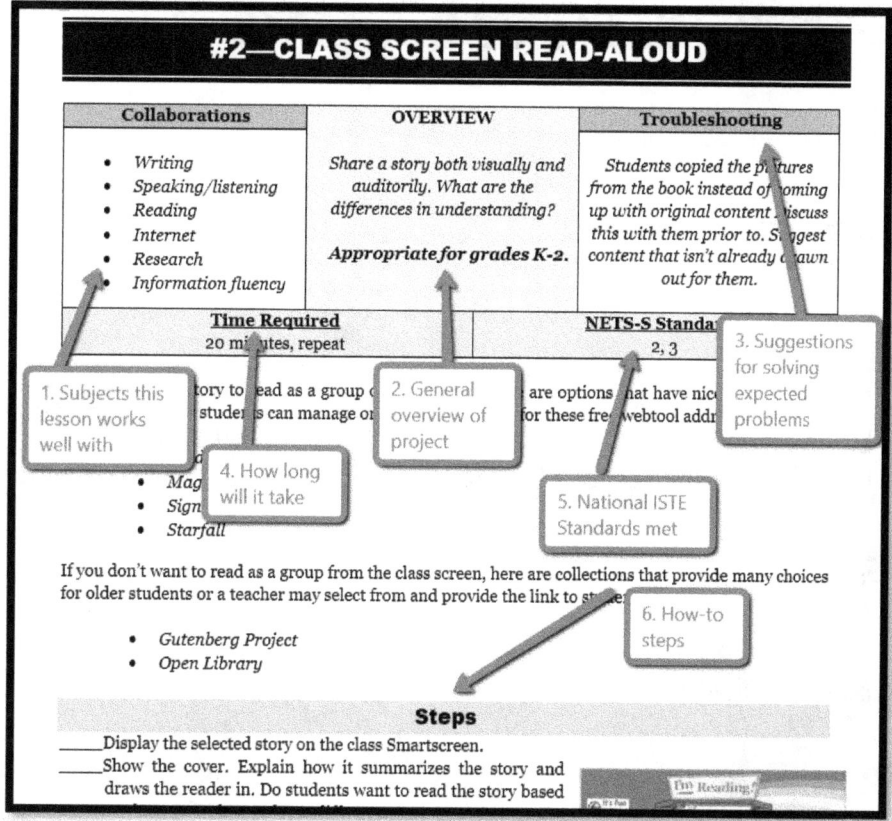

1. **Collaborations**—Core classes this lesson supports
2. **Overview**—Quick summary of project
3. **Troubleshooting**—How to solve expected problems—if there are any
4. **Time Required**—how long to budget for this project
5. **ISTE Standards**—This highlights which ISTE standards are delivered with the lesson.
6. **Steps**—practical strategies for achieving essential goals with step-by-step guidelines

We've included blanks in front of each step so you can check it off when completed. The nature of educational technology often precludes completing an activity in one sitting. It's useful to track where you ended so you can pick up there when you continue.

About the Authors

Ask a Tech Teacher is an award-winning resource blog run by a group of technology teachers offering resources, advice, lesson plans, pedagogical conversation, website reviews, newsletters, and more. It's a favorite of teachers looking to maneuver the minefields of tech in education.

Jacqui Murray has been teaching K-18 technology for 30 years. She is the editor/author of over a hundred tech ed resources including a K-12 technology curriculum, K-8 keyboard curriculum, K-8 Digital Citizenship curriculum. She is an adjunct professor in tech ed, Master Teacher, webmaster for four blogs, an Amazon Vine Voice, freelance journalist on tech ed topics, and contributor to NEA Today. You can find her resources at Structured Learning.

Table of Contents

Kindergarten
- Talking Pictures
- Class Screen Read-aloud
- Practice Letters on the Internet
- Mouse Practice
- Shape Stroll

1st Grade
- Picture the Details
- Brainstorm Ideas
- How do I Keyboard in First Grade?
- What's a Digital Citizen?
- I am a Puzzle

2nd Grade
- QR Me
- Why is Digital Privacy Important?
- How to Animoto
- Life Cycle Reports
- How to Keyboard in 2nd Grade

3rd Grade
- Compare With Venn Diagrams
- Puzzle Maker to Prepare for Tests
- Create a Timeline of Events
- How to Survive on Landforms
- How To Avoid Cyberbullying

4th Grade
- How do I Keyboard in 4th Grade?
- What is Digital Citizenship?
- Classify Animals Like a Pro
- Book Reviews by the Characters
- IPads 101

5th Grade
- Scratch for Fifth Graders
- Digital Citizens and Internet Safety
- Tessellations Around the World
- Google Earth Literary Tour

6th Grade
- Digital Citizenship 101
- Twitter in Education
- Formulas in Spreadsheets
- Keyboarding: Touch Typing
- Digital Posters

Kindergarten

#1—TALKING PICTURES

Collaborations	OVERVIEW	Troubleshooting
• Internet • Literature • Science • Speaking • Writing	*Blend image with voice to share ideas.* **Appropriate for grades K-6 with adaptations**	Can't get the app to work correctly? *Try a different browser. This is a good troubleshooting solution for anything web-based.*
Time Required 30 minutes		**ISTE Standards** 1, 2, 5, 6

Examples of talking picture webtools. If you can't find these by Googling the website, visit Ask a Tech Teacher and their Images resource page:

- *Chatterpix*
- *PicSay*
- *Talk-n-Photos*
- *Tapikeo*
- *Thinglink*
- *Voki*

Steps

_____ If this is one of the first times students have used the internet, explain how it works. Point out the toolbars, the 'back' button, the 'home' button, the address bar, the scroll bar. Let students get comfortable with their use before beginning this project.

_____ Have enough adult supervision to help students when they get stuck. Nothing's more frustrating than wanting to complete a project and waiting what seems like forever for assistance.

_____ Walk students through the layout of the program you plan to use. Demonstrate the project so they visualize the steps.

_____ Prior to the unit's start, each student selects an ocean animal, finds a digital picture of it, and saves it to their file folder.

_____ As you study the unit in class, each student notes three-four facts about the animal they selected. At the end, review each animal with the class and list the discussed facts on the class screen.

_____ Students can work in groups of 2-3 on this project.

_____ Upload the image to be used to the webtool or app being used. If it's an animal, in Chatterpix, students will select parts of the mouth so it appears to be talking.

_____ Review what was learned about the animal. Have the student (each one in the group or a volunteer) practice the presentation. Available adults can remind them of the salient points if they get stuck.

_____ Tape himself/herself/themselves as though they were the animal. For example, "I am a whale. I weigh 2 tons..."

_____Once students have all presentation pieces collected (the image, the dialogue, the recording if they're uploading an audio file), it takes less than five minutes to complete.
_____When all students are done, ask students to reflect on this activity.
_____Presentations can be exported to the student digital portfolio or class website for all to enjoy.

Extensions:

Have (older) students use Voki to be an historical figure from a unit they are studying and explain their rationale for what they did that made them memorable. For even older students, use Thinglink to explain the stand of a political candidate,

This is great for differentiation—to allow visual students to provide evidence of their learning in ways best suited to their learning style.

Notes

#2—CLASS SCREEN READ-ALOUD

Collaborations	OVERVIEW	Troubleshooting
• Internet • Reading • Research • Speaking/listening • Writing	*Share a story both visually and auditorily. What are the differences in understanding?* *Appropriate for grades K-2.*	Students copied the pictures from the book instead of coming up with original content *Discuss this with them. Suggest content that isn't already drawn.*
Time Required 20 minutes, repeat		**ISTE Standards** 2, 3

Examples of online books webtools. If you can't find these by Googling the website, visit Ask a Tech Teacher Reading resource page:

- *Kinder Stories*
- *Signed Stories (app)*
- *Starfall*

If you don't want to read as a group from the class screen, here are collections that provide many choices for older students or a teacher may select and provide the link to students:

- *Gutenberg Project*
- *Open Library*

Steps

____Display the selected story on the class screen.

____Show the cover. Explain how it summarizes the story and draws the reader in. Do students want to read the story based on the cover? If not, select a different one.

____Show the back cover (if any). How does it add to the overall understanding and interest in the story? (For older grades: Is there a Table of Contents? An index? What do these contribute?)

____Point out the author. Have students read other stories by this author? Take this opportunity to discuss what it means to be published. Introduce the idea of 'plagiarism' and 'copyright protections' in an age-appropriate manner.

____Read part of the story modeling emphasis, dialogue, various characters. Pay attention to grammar (pauses for commas, periods, semi-colons; voice rises for question mark; voice excited for exclamation point).

____Have students take turns reading to the class, modeling your delivery.

_____Pause when students have difficulty with a word or mispronounce it. Discuss prefixes and suffixes (age appropriate) that will help students decode a word.

_____Show students how included pictures can help them determine the meaning of a confusing word. Explain the concept of 'multi-media'.

_____When completed, have students come up to class screen and point out different characters, actions, plot items, and setting details.

_____Ask students to draw pictures to accompany the text to help other readers better understand the story. Students can use KidPix, TuxPaint, or another drawing program.

_____Ask students to think about the messages conveyed by the images, the text, and the auditory story? What is the same? What are differences? Which do they prefer? Or do they like a combination?

_____When done, add student images to class website.

_____Have (older) students visit each other's pictures and share comments if the program allows.

Extensions:

Ask students questions about the story. Have them point to the part of the text that they used to answer the question, using the story as displayed on the class screen.

Visit Ask a Tech Teacher and select from their reading resources (many free).

Notes

_____
_____
_____
_____
_____
_____
_____
_____
_____

#3—Practice Letters on the Internet

Collaborations	OVERVIEW	Troubleshooting
• Communication • Information fluency • Reading • Research • Writing	Students review letters and words learned in class by participating in activities on letter/word websites *Appropriate for grades K,1*	How do I prevent students from rushing through stories? *Read the story silently, then engage students in a conversation.*

Time Required	ISTE Standards
20 minutes, repeat	2, 3

Examples of webtools that teach letters to students. If you can't find these by Googling the website, visit Ask a Tech Teacher and their Letters resource page:

- *Alphabetimals—learn the alphabet with animal sounds*
- *Find the letter—easy, medium, hard*
- *Fischer Price Learning Letters (app)*
- *GeoGreeting*
- *Learn Letters with Max (video)*
- *Learn Letters (app)*
- *Starfall Letters*
- *Spin and Spot Safari — explore letters through a safari (app)*

Steps

____Have sufficient helpers when using online websites. This is particularly important for young users who are easily frustrated.

____Review letters in the order they are introduced in the classroom by showing them on the class screen.

____Discuss what 'letter' means. What happens when they are combined? What is their importance in words? Sentences? Paragraphs and stories?

____List letter recognition websites on the class internet start page so students can access them with a click.

____List letters students will work with in class to avoid confusion. For example, if students start with c, o, a, d, and g, list those.

____Demo each website on the class start page so younger students will be comfortable using them.

____This activity is self-directed. Students work as independently as possible. Encourage students to trace the

letters with their finger on the screen, say them out loud, notice space between words and upper/lower case. When ready, students can count syllables.

____If this is students' first time on the internet, review basics before beginning: how to select a link, how to go back to where they were, how to use tabbed internet to toggle between websites, how to use *Favorites* (if appropriate).

____Remind students of best practices for internet use: never click ads, stay on the appropriate website, use tab on internet toolbar to return to main page.

____When students are ready to move on to words, use the class screen to share (these can be found by searching your internet browser or visiting Ask a Tech Teacher's Reading resource page):

- *Aesop Fables—no ads*
- *Aesop's Fables*
- *Audio stories*
- *Classic Fairy Tales*
- *Fairy Tales and Fables*
- *Listen/read–Free non-fic audio books*
- *Owl Eyes (classics)*
- *Starfall*
- *Stories read by actors*
- *Stories to read for youngsters*
- *Storyline*
- *Unite for Literacy*

or your favorite site. See the list in a prior lesson.

____Follow words from left to right, top to bottom, and page by page. Recognize that spoken words are represented in a written language with a specific sequence of letters. Understand that words are separated by spaces when printed. Recognize and name upper- and lowercase letters.

____Have students follow a sentence on the screen with their finger. Point out the space between words and the punctuation after a sentence.

____Encourage students to work independently. They can read aloud (in a whisper) if this helps.

____Discuss their thoughts as a group or with the class. What was different about digital books from a traditional print book? What did they like less? More? Why?

Extensions:

Have students read stories by themselves, without you joining them on the class screen. If they start one they don't like, they can move on to another choice.

Visit Ask a Tech Teacher and select from their reading resources (many free).

Inquiry-based Teaching with PBL

#4—MOUSE PRACTICE

Collaborations	OVERVIEW	Troubleshooting
• Reading • Speaking/listening • Technology skills • Writing	New computer users learn good mouse habits. ***Appropriate for grades K-4 with adaptations***	*Spend time during each lesson correcting hand position on the mouse. They'll get used to it and it'll be habit soon, but not right away.*
Time Required 5 minutes, repeat for several classes		**ISTE Standards** 6

Examples of mouse practice webtools. If you can't find these by Googling the website, visit Ask a Tech Teacher's Mouse Skills resource page:

- *Drawing Melody—create music with mouse*
- *Fischer Price Let's Play Piano*
- *Macmillan Mouse and tech basics—video*
- *Bomomo Mouse practice—drag, click*
- *MouseProgram*
- *My Computer Mouse—video and song*
- *OwlieBoo—mouse practice*
- *Wack-a-gopher (no gophers hurt in this)*

Steps

____Mouse use for new computer students isn't intuitive. It requires explanation and reinforcement for students to understand.

____Demonstrate to kindergarteners the correct way to hold the mouse: 1) the pointer (index finger) is on the left mouse button, 2) the middle finger is on the right mouse button, 3) thumb is on left side of mouse, 4) palm is on bottom of mouse. Walk around and make sure students are all holding the mouse correctly.

____Be sensitive to the fact that kindergartners barely know right from left. If they get it wrong, correct gently. I often say, "The other left" to indicate the other side. Also be sensitive that their hands are small on a full-sized mouse. That's OK. They'll get used to it.

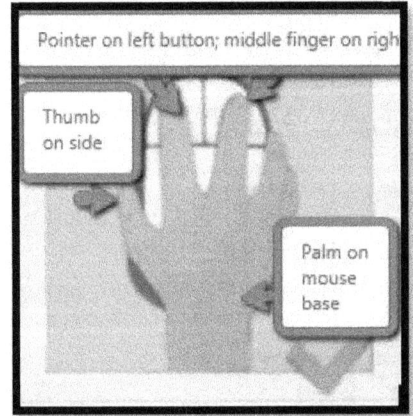

____Show students how their station is set up: 1) keyboard directly in front of them, directly in front of the monitor, 2) mouse to the right (or left, for lefties) of the keyboard.

____Students who are left handed may use the mouse the traditional way or you may set up the mouse for them on the left side of the keyboard. Find out what parents do at home and synchronize.

____Discuss the mouse button. Have them click the left one. Let them know they won't use the right mouse button until next year or the year after

____Have them click the right-mouse button on a program (maybe the internet) to see that it invokes a drop-down menu with lots of words

____Have them experiment with the mouse wheel. It rolls. Put in on a page and see how they go up and down the page. Relate that to the scroll bar on the right side of the screen.

____Explain terminology for mouse skills: 1) click means to push the left mouse button, 2) right-click means to click the right mouse button (again, they won't need that skill this year), 3) scroll means to roll the mouse wheel and move up and down the page, 4) drag-and-drop means to click the left mouse button and move the mouse. Have them try all of these.

____Before beginning mouse practice, do finger exercises to encourage use of all fingers. You can find these exercises in lessons on Keyboarding.

____Done? Have students visit several of the mouse websites listed at the start of the lesson to get started on mouse skills. I spend twenty minutes per class, for 3-4 classes on this while I troll the room and make sure hand positions are correct. These mouse programs cover basic mouse skills: 1) click, 2) double click, 3) drag-and-drop, 4) mouse wheel

MOUSE CONTROL

Single Click:
Select

Double Click:
Open

Right Click:
Drop-down menu

Extension:

Practice an age-appropriate keyboarding program like Type to Learn Jr. This mixes keyboarding and mouse skills so will get students used to how mouse skills are integrated into computer use.

Notes

Inquiry-based Teaching with PBL

#5—Shape Stroll

Collaborations	OVERVIEW	Troubleshooting
• Critical thinking • Reading • Speaking/listening • Writing	*Students take a stroll around school or the classroom to discover shapes discussed during class.* **Appropriate for grades K-2**	Some students can't stay focused on finding shapes. That's OK. You'll probably have enough with other students' discoveries

Time Required	ISTE Standards
30 minutes	1, 4

Examples of webtools for drawing. If you can't find these by Googling the website, visit Ask a Tech Teacher and the Art-Drawing resource page:

- *ABCYa Paint–great for Chromebooks*
- *Draw and Tell by Duck Duck Moose (app)*
- *Draw.to*
- *Doodle Cast–fee (app)*
- *Draw–for K-2 (app)*
- *Drawp– with school accounts (app)*
- *KidPix Deluxe 3D–fee (app)*
- *SumoPaint–no log-in; good with Chromebooks*
- *Wixie–with your Wixie (or Pixie) subscription (app)*

Steps

____Review two-dimensional and three-dimensional shapes with students—squares, circles, triangles, rectangles, hexagons, cubes, cones, cylinders, spheres. Draw them on the class screen.

____Point out examples of shapes in the classroom—the class screen is a rectangle, the Welcome sign is a triangle, etc.

____Discuss structures around school that the students can think of. Is there a triangle, square, rectangle, etc., as part of them?

____Have sufficient helpers during this exercise—at least one parent for each ten students—to help with discovery and recording.

____Walk around the school (with sufficient assistance to supervise properly) and ask students to point out where they see squares, rectangles, circles, diamonds, cubes, pyramids and other shapes discussed in class. Write them down as students call them out.

_____Show students how orientation and spatial relationship isn't always what the student is used to seeing—i.e., a triangle might be resting on its point or a rectangle on its long side.

_____Can students find structures around school that are a combination of two or more shapes? Help students delineate how multiple shapes work together to create one image.

_____Return to the classroom and list the shapes found on the overhead or class screen. Ask students to remind you where they saw them (the front of the building, a ball, etc.). Jog their memories if necessary.

_____Discuss what it means that their school has so many of the shapes they study in math class. What conclusions can they draw from that?

_____Open KidPix (purchased software), TuxPaint (free downloadable software), Paint (free with Windows), or the class drawing program. Have students recall the shapes they saw during the Shapes Stroll. Visualize it in situ. Have students share with the class how it fit into a three-dimensional structure (if appropriate).

_____Have students draw one of the shapes and then draw the surrounding item—building, play structure, window, etc.

_____Add their name to picture. Export and print. Upload to class website or wiki to share.

_____Ask students to reflect on this activity. What did they learn? What did they like/dislike about it? Explain why.

Extension:

Ask students to visualize their neighborhood, home, or room. What shapes do they see in their mind's eye? Can they draw those shapes and the structures around them?

If you can't go outside, have students use shapes found around the classroom.

Have students use their descriptive writing skills to describe what they have drawn, how math shapes are the basis for the physical world.

Have students draw their name with shapes.

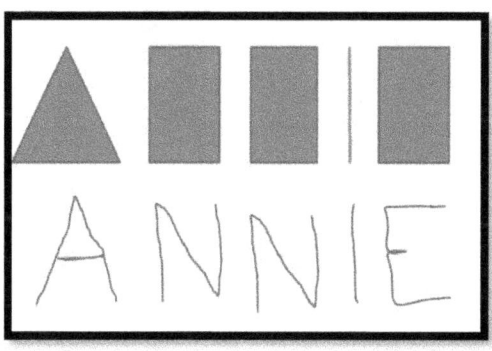

First Grade

#1—Picture the Details

Collaborations	OVERVIEW	Troubleshooting
• Communication • Critical Thinking • Reading/Writing	Students learn to follow directions as they add detail to a picture and visually tell a story.	If this takes too long or frustrates some students, it can be done in groups.
Time Required 45 minutes		**ISTE Standards** 2, 4

Examples of webtools for drawing If you can't find these by Googling the website, visit Ask a Tech Teacher and the Art–Drawing resource page:

- ABCYa Paint–great for Chromebooks
- Draw and Tell by Duck Duck Moose (app)
- Draw.to
- Doodle Cast–fee (app)
- Draw–for K-2 (app)
- Drawp– with school accounts (app)
- KidPix Deluxe 3D–fee (app)
- SumoPaint–no log-in required; good with Chromebooks
- Wixie–with your existing Wixie (or Pixie) subscription (app)

Steps

_____This lesson sharpens auditory and visual skills such as:

- Listening for understanding
- Following directions
- Following directions the first time given
- Paying sustained attention
- Problem-solving
- Knowing how to ask for help

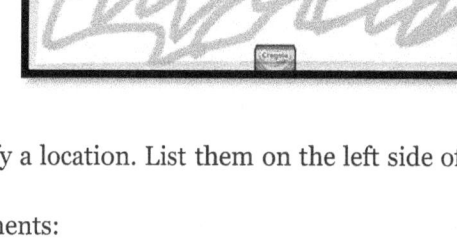

_____Before beginning, discuss each of these direction-following skills. What does it mean to 'listen for understanding'? To pay 'sustained attention'? Demonstrate each for students.
_____On the class screen, draw a line down the middle.
_____Ask students what types of details would help them identify a location. List them on the left side of the class screen.
_____Remind students these details must follow certain requirements:

- They must be sequential—certain details must be in place before others can be added.

- They must be spatial—placed correctly in the big picture.
- They must be quantitative—knowing a house has three windows is important.

____Ask clarifying questions as needed to develop a comprehensive list of details to identify a setting.

____On the right side of the screen, draw a picture with each detail in the order students tell you is spatially correct. Ask clarifying questions to get details accurate.

____Erase what you've drawn. Return to the left side—the one that lists what students considered important to identify a location. Ask students to think about [insert the name of a story they've read in class]. Consider the setting in terms of this list. For example, a house.

____On the right side of the class screen, draw each detail in the order students tell you is spatially correct. Ask clarifying questions to get the details accurate. For example, where are the windows? Are they open or closed?

____When done, have students open their drawing program.

____Ask them to think of another setting in the story and draw it using the list developed on the left side of the class screen.

____When they are done, ask them to reflect on this exercise. What was difficult, easy? What did they learn?

____Put all pictures on class website as part of the story's literacy unit.

Extension:

Do this backwards: Draw the picture and ask students to describe the details that went into creating it.

Notes

_____
_____
_____
_____
_____
_____
_____
_____

#2—Brainstorm Ideas

Collaborations	OVERVIEW	Troubleshooting
• Critical thinking • Reading • Speaking/listening • Technology operations • Writing	Students create a colorful mind map to organize information on a topic. **Appropriate for grades 1-5 with variations.**	It's difficult to create the bubble by dragging in Bubbl.us. *I agree, which is one reason I prefer others.*
Time Required 30 minutes (2 sessions)		**ISTE Standards** 1, 2, 4

Examples of webtools for fairy tales. If you can't find these by Googling the website, visit Ask a Tech Teacher and the Reading resource page:

- *Aesop's Fables—audio/visual*
- *Children's Stories—MagicKey*

These are examples of mindmapping webtools. If you can't find the website by Googling, visit Ask a Tech Teacher's Visual Learning-Mindmaps resource page:

- *Bubbl.us*
- *Google Draw*
- *iMindmap*
- *iMindQ*
- *Inspiration*
- *Mind42*
- *MindMaple*
- *Popplet*
- *Spiderscribe*

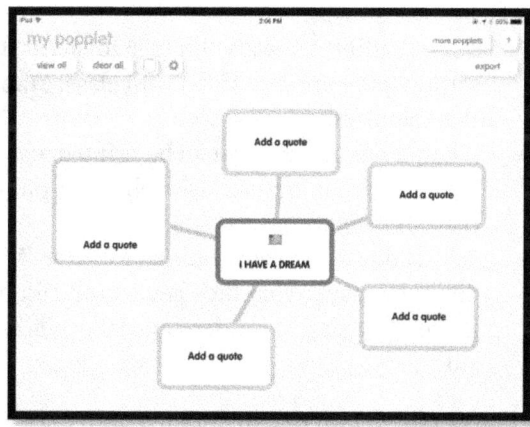

Steps

_____ Have sufficient helpers when using technology with youngers who get frustrated more easily by problems and questions.

_____ This is a summative activity. In this case, it follows a unit on fairy tales but it could be any inquiry unit that includes a central theme and supporting facts.

_____ Students read a variety of fairy tales in class. Discuss specific elements of each, for example, main characters, setting and conclusion.

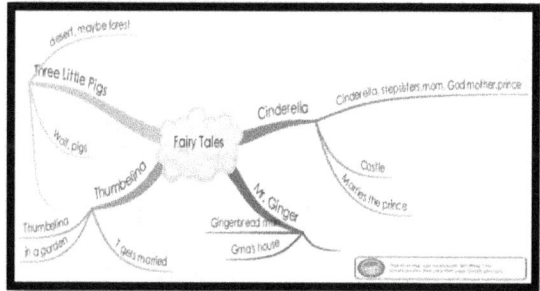

_____Open a brainstorming program on the class screen. 'Brainstorming' helps students work as a group to expand on ideas and think critically about a subject.

_____Type a central idea in the middle bubble—in this case, 'fairy tales'. Ask students to collaboratively name fairy tales read as a class. Add each as an arm around the center (in this case, *Cinderella, Mr. Ginger, Three Little Pigs,* and *Thumbelina*). Have students pick colors and suggest the arrangement of the child bubbles so they are easily viewed.

_____Discuss concepts like 'main character', 'setting', 'plot', 'crisis'. As students identify these, add them as 'child bubbles'.

_____Ask students to share what they remember about each of these concepts and add them as sub-bubbles to their child bubble.

_____Continue until students run out of details. Add colors. Vary the look of the arms. Insert images. Format to make the map clear and appealing.

_____Leave mind map on class screen while students read additional fairy tales online from a list available on the class website.

_____Ask students to think about the details mapped for the first stories.

_____Done reading? Ask a volunteer to share the name of their story and three details (main character, setting, plot, and/or crisis) with class. Map it as they talk. If you have a class screen, have students do this themselves.

_____When done, mind map can be printed, exported or saved. Share it on the class website or publish it to the class wiki.

_____Ask students to reflect on this exercise. What was difficult, easy? What did they learn? Did mapping make it easier to understand the pieces of the story?

Extension:

Have students work in groups to create a mind map of their own on another topic connected to classroom inquiry. When done, publish them to the class website as part of the unit's discussion.

#3—How do I Keyboard in First Grade?

Collaborations	OVERVIEW	Troubleshooting
• Anything requiring typing • Literature • Writing	Students begin keyboarding instruction in a fun, age-appropriate way.	Students use the wrong finger. *Don't expect the right finger until third grade. Concentrate on posture, hands on keyboard, elbows at sides.*
Time Required 15 minutes, repeat		**ISTE Standards** 6

Examples of keyboarding webtools. If you can't find these by Googling the website, visit Ask a Tech Teacher and the Keyboarding resource page:

- *ABCYa Keyboard Challenge*
- *Alphabet rain game*
- *Barracuda game*
- *Brown Bear Typing (Learn to Type)*
- *Bubbles game*
- *Type Dojo*
- *Type to Learn Jr.*

Steps

_____Keyboarding is a **cumulative skill**. What can be effectively learned at one level depends heavily upon what was learned earlier. If hunt 'n peck habits become ingrained, it is difficult to become a touch typist.

_____If this is the first keyboard class for your students, take a tour of the keyboard with them. Point out the following:

- *Enter—what's this used for?*
- *Space bar—what's it used for?*
- *Caps lock and shift—what's the difference?*
- *Backspace and delete—what's the difference?*
- *Tab—what's this used for?*
- *Home row—why is this row important?*
- *Top row with numbers*
- *Ctrl, Alt keys—share some age-appropriate uses of these two keys*

_____Start with finger warm-ups. These show students that they have five fingers, that all of them work, that some are stronger than others. Here are four, all age-appropriate for youngers:

Warm up Fingers
- Lay your hand flat on a table (in the inset, the book doubles as the table) with all fingers touching. Spread your fingers apart as far as possible and hold for three seconds. Close fingers together. Repeat 10 times.

- Next, lift each finger and move it around, then lower it. One at a time until you've exercised each.

Stretch Fingers
- Hold hands facing each other. Touch the thumb from your right hand to the thumb of your left hand. Touch the first finger on your right hand to the first finger on the left hand. Repeat until all fingers are touching.

- With fingers pressed together, pull palms away from each other creating a cup shape with fingers and palm. Starting at the finger tips, slowly move palms closer together, rolling the pressure down the fingers until all four fingers are pressed together. Hold for 10 seconds. Move back to the starting position and repeat 10 times.

Aerobics for Fingers
- Hold hand in the air with fingers spread apart so it looks like a "high-five." Move just the thumb to the palm and press. Bring the thumb back out to the starting position and move the first finger to the palm and press. Move the first finger back to the starting position and repeat slowly with the remaining fingers. Fingers not pressing into the palm should be held as straight as possible.

- After one round, try again a little faster. Repeat 10 times, increasing speed with each round.

Weight Training for Fingers
- Grab a scrap piece of paper and crumble it into a ball with one hand. Squeeze the paper ball tightly and hold for 10 seconds. Repeat with the other hand.

_____Have students sit at keyboard:

- *Sit straight, square, centered to the keyboard, feet flat on floor*
- *Use proper distance from the keyboard*
- *Keep elbows close to sides*
- *Keep fingers slightly curved (think: cat claws, not dog paws)*

_____Open software or online keyboarding webtool. Rotate these programs throughout the year so students don't get tired of any one.

_____Start with Brown Bear typing to concentrate on **letter location only**. Explain that once they remember key placement, they get faster at all keyboarding.

_____In Brown Bear, I set a goal for students (say, 28 points—this reflects keys typed, not wpm) that they must reach before moving on to whatever the next activity is in class. Every five minutes, I lower that goal so eventually all students achieve it. I continually remind them that this is all about remembering where the keys are. Students love this program! It is an oft-requested activity. I give a crown out to each student who beats the fastest score in the grade level for the year. For example, last year, our top score got to 46, with five crowns awarded throughout the year!

_____Keep keyboarding fun and light, but help students develop good habits they'll need in the future when speed and accuracy become important.

Extension:

Set up several of the online programs on different computers throughout the lab. Have students spend ten minutes at each station, then switch to a new program.

What Should You Expect of Younger Keyboarders?

Before I answer that question, let's answer a more fundamental question: Should you expect youngers to keyboard? I'm talking about students between kindergarten and fifth grade. Are they mature enough? Do they have the fine motor skills required to use the pinkie to push the A key? Do they have the necessary focus and concentration?

The answer is a resounding Yes, though when I reviewed the literature on this subject, it is all over the place as far as when students should/could begin to focus on speed and accuracy. Some say third grade; some say not until fifth or sixth.

From my experience, it's third grade, though I teach pre-keyboard skills as young as kindergarten. That might be why my students are ready in third grade.

Here's a caveat: **You'll have to be the arbiter of what is true for your group. If you determine your students aren't ready, wait a year.** You're the teacher. You'll know when they're ready.

Once you decide, the next question is: How do I do it? Here's a quick answer. Prepare kindergarteners by teaching pre-keyboard skills like posture, hand placement, mouse skills, and some shortkeys. This gives their young brains and their immature fine motor skills time to develop. When you determine they're ready, move on to speed and accuracy.

#4—What's a Digital Citizen?

Collaborations	OVERVIEW	Troubleshooting
• Reading • Research	Students learn to live in the world of websites, copyrighted images, and friends who may be something different. *Appropriate for grades K, 1*	Students still click outside of the assigned website. Yes, but with diligence, they will come to understand the right way.

Time Required	ISTE Standards
15 minutes, repeat	5

Examples of cyberbullying webtools. If you can't find these by Googling the website, visit Ask a Tech Teacher and the Digital Citizens-Cyberbully resource page:

- *Cyberbullying–You're not Alone – Hector's World*
- *Cyberbullying–* (access BrainPOP with ed account and search for topic)
- *Cyberbullying–what is it*
- *Think Time: How Does Cyberbullying Affect You--a hard-hitting short video that hits all important points*
- *What is Cyberbullying? from Commonsense Media*

Examples of netiquette webtools. If you can't find these by Googling the website, visit Ask a Tech Teacher and the Digital Citizens-netiquette resource page:

- *Discussion Board Netiquette – video*
- *Netiquette – made in Powtoons*
- *Netiquette for beginners – video*
- *Netiquette: Playing Nice on the Web – video*
- *Teacher's Guide to Netiquette*

Steps

_____The objectives for this lesson include:

- Understand that computers can be used to visit far-away places and learn new things.
- Understand that staying safe online is similar to staying safe in the real world.
- Describe how to travel safely on the internet.

____Gather students on the class rug and discuss the meaning of '**digital citizen**'. How is this the same/different from being a citizen of the town they live in? Where is this 'digital town'?

____As a town has rules and laws, so does the digital world. Discuss what these are? Why are they important?

____What are the rights and responsibilities of being a 'digital citizen', even as a first grader? For example, when they find pictures they like on the internet, does the creator of that picture have rights? Does the user have responsibilities?

____Discuss the potential risks and dangers associated with online communications.

____What is '**netiquette**'? Discuss internet etiquette as it relates to a first grader. Access some of the websites listed above (either search them on the internet or find them on the Ask a Tech Teacher website resources).

____What is **cyberbullying**? Do any students know someone who's been bullied? Why is that bad? How would that relate to the online world? Access some of the websites listed above (either search them on the internet or find them on the Ask a Tech Teacher website resources).

____Keep these conversations to 10-15 minutes. Solicit student ideas. Help them understand that the virtual world is not safe just because they can't see it—but it can be a healthy place to explore and learn.

____Have students return to their seats and log onto the computer. Discuss why they use a **password** to access the computer.

____Bring up a website (one you use in class). Show students how to correctly use it:

- *Don't click on other websites (how can they identify those)*
- *Don't click on ads (what is an ad).*
- *Distinguish ads from content on sites.*

____Visit videos that teach online safety. Here are options--Access these either by searching them on the internet or finding them on the Ask a Tech Teacher digital citizenship resources:

- *Internet safety video–day in a digital citizen's life*
- *My Online Neighborhood–video by CommonSense Media*
- *NetSafety–a series of videos on internet safety; varied age groups; well-done*
- *Safety Land game*

____Go over the summation of good digital citizenship (see inset). Zoom in if needed.

Extension:

Gather students back on class rug and reflect on what they saw in the videos. How did it make them feel? What did they learn?

> Don't talk to strangers. Look both ways before crossing the (virtual) street. Don't go places you don't know. Play fair. Pick carefully who you trust. Don't get distracted by bling. And sometimes, stop everything and take a nap.

#5—I am a Puzzle

Collaborations	OVERVIEW	Troubleshooting
• Art • Critical thinking • Writing	*Visually represent who the first grade student is and how s/he fits into the Big Picture*	The pieces don't fit together well. *(That's OK. Isn't that the way life is?)*
Time Required 30 minutes (2 sessions		**ISTE Standards** 2, 6

Examples of drawing webtools. If you can't find these by Googling the website, visit Ask a Tech Teacher and the Art-Drawing resource page:

- *ABCYa Paint*
- *Doodle Buddy*
- *GIMP*
- *KidPix*
- *TuxPaint*

Steps

____Nothing makes first graders happier than sharing who they are. Use that to facilitate technology practice, writing skills, and art while creating a visual quilt of your class.

____Why a puzzle piece? Discuss this with students. Who are they? What do they remember that made a big difference in their lives? The arrival of a sibling? The death of a beloved dog? The school they went to? Aren't most memories when they are part of something else? Discuss how who they are is a culmination of many decisions, many activities, small and large.

____Extend the discussion to the class. It is made up of all children. What it is depends upon who they are daily. Last year's first grade class was different because of its unique mix of students.

____This can be an opportunity for serious discussions on behavior issues, disagreements among students, cultural clashes that are otherwise sensitive to discuss with first graders.

____Create the puzzle piece template from your favorite drawing program. You can fill it with a solid color, color in it, or add a texture. There are also many shapes. You can create one of each and let students choose which they want.

____Save as a .jpg to student network folder.

____Have each student open the template in the school drawing program.

_____Draw a picture of themselves using the drawing program's art tools. Discuss mouse use as they draw and the need to click, drag, drag-and-drop to make the pencil or paint brush work.
_____Save to network folders and print.
_____Cut the puzzle pieces out. Paste them on your classroom wall in a shape your students select (like the tree in the inset). It can be a traditional quilt, a border of interlinking pieces around the classroom, or an object.
_____When done, ask students to reflect on this. What did they learn?

Extension:

Adjust pieces throughout the year to reflect seasons, class events, holidays, or whatever suits the class.

Besides the picture, add one sentence about who they are and one sentence about what they like in first grade (or pick a topic that fits your classroom discussion).

Have students make multiple puzzle pieces with snippets of information about themselves. Print individual quilts of what suits each child.

Create a bulletin board with all puzzle pieces displayed. I do this on a door in the classroom, shape it like a student and call it the 'Computer Student'.

Notes

Second Grade

#1—QR Me

Collaborations	OVERVIEW	Troubleshooting
• Listening • Reading • Research • Speaking • Writing	Students write elements of a story and insert as a QR code into for others. *Appropriate for grades 2-6 with adaptations*	The QR scanner doesn't work. *The QR code must have no errors. Check to be sure no part is cut off or painted over.*
Time Required 30 minutes (2 sessions)		**ISTE Standards** 1, 2

Examples of QR Code webtools. If you can't find these by Googling, visit Ask a Tech Teacher resource pages:

- GoQR
- Kaywa
- QR Stuff

Step

____QR Codes (Quick Response Codes) are like barcodes, similar to those you see on almost every product you buy. The main difference is that QR Codes can store much more data and more complex data in a smaller surface area. The Code itself is an image file that can be copied, pasted, embedded, downloaded, and uploaded — anything you normally do to an image file.

____The only risk about QR Codes is they aren't readable by humans. So, be careful that you check each before posting it.

____Discuss the importance of questions like who, what, when, where, why, how. What do they mean? How do the answers demonstrate an understanding of key details? How do they describe actions, thoughts, feelings, signal event order and provide a sense of closure?

____Use a story all students have read to show how answering six questions provides a complete elaboration of an event or sequence of events, including sensory details, action, descriptive details, and temporal words that help to provide a sense of order and closure to a narrative.

____Using a story the student has just finished, write out answers to these questions. If several students read the same book, have them collaborate on answers. Answers will become a QR code.

____Discuss 'QR codes'. They are created by an app and then scanned with a smart phone or QR Reader that decodes what's written and does what is instructed. Sometimes, it shows simple text. Other times, it takes you to a website, shows a picture, or plays a video.

____Where have students seen them? Have examples from stores and magazines available to show. What is the benefit of this approach (lots of information in a small space, can provide a direct link to a website without having to type in the complicated address)?

_____Open a QR creator available on the internet (such as the ones listed at the beginning of this lesson). Most are simple enough for a second grader to use. Decide what type of QR Code you'll use. This will vary by the app you select. The insets show examples of what is available. Zoom in if necessary.

_____First, type the title of the book being reviewed, followed by the answers to the six questions—*who, what, when, where, why, how*. If you don't answer that many questions in your 2nd grade, skip those that aren't relevant. If the answers are created in a Word file (as suggested in the *Extension*), have students open that file and copy-paste text into the QR Creator.

_____As they type, students will see the QR code develop. The more information they add, the denser are the black-and-white squiggles. What else do students notice about the QR Code (for example, what's with the corners?)

_____Have students check their work to be sure all the questions are answered.

_____Once the QR code is created, save to student file folder (via online tool or take a screen shot and save).

_____Import it into the class drawing program (you can get ideas of drawing programs from Ask a Tech Teacher's *Art/Drawing* resource page) and draw one of the book's characters around the QR Code (see inset). Be sure not to overlap any of the black lines because then the QR Code won't be readable.

_____Print the QR Code and insert it into the book with help of the librarian.

_____QR codes must be complete. Don't allow any extraneous pieces and be sure the entire code is copied (see QR Person inset for example of what NOT to do—the QR code is slightly colored over by the skirt and will not work).

_____Show students how to use the Camera on the smart phone (if available) or the Scan app on iPads or Smartphones to read the QR data. Give students lots of time to scan classmates' codes. They find this pretty cool. Anything that gets students reading about books, thoughtfully selecting one they like and based on their own research, is a good thing in second grade.

_____When done, ask them to reflect on this exercise. What was difficult, easy? What did they learn?

_____You may want to encourage the librarian to have iPads available with a QR Scanner so students can read the summary of the book in this manner.

Extension:

Have students type answers (using good grammar and spelling) into Word as an intro to word processing. Then, show students how to copy-paste it from Word into the QR creator.

Post QR codes in the library corner of the classroom. Students can scan them for ideas on which book they'd like to read.

Have students draw a picture of themselves or a character in the book around the QR code using school drawing program.

Holiday project? Have students put their Santa list on the QR code with hints for parents as to what they want.

Use a special program called QR Voice to translate the QR code into an audio file that plays when you use the QR scanner. This is particularly exciting for Language B teachers. Turn class vocabulary or projects into the spoken word so students can hear an authentic representation of the language.

Record students reading a short story and embed it into a QR Code. Post these on a gallery in your classroom where students can stop and visit anytime for a quick story read by their classmates.

Have students follow a QR Code scavenger hunt to find all the important places in the school (with their parents if you do it for Back to School Night). That makes all that information available on their phones for later use.

Notes

#2—Why is Digital Privacy Important?

Collaborations	OVERVIEW	Troubleshooting
• Internet use • Research • Social skills	Students take the lessons about digital citizenship learned in first grade and expand them to digital privacy and digital rights	Student upset over what they see. Preview material. If something happens, discuss it with child. Maybe they skip it.
Time Required 15-30 minutes, several		**ISTE Standards** 1, 6

Copyright-free images. If you can't find these by Googling the website, visit Ask a Tech Teacher and the Images resource page:

- *Creative Commons*
- *Free Photo*
- *Google Images (adapt to your student grade level)*
- *Open Photo*
- *Photos for Class*
- *Smithsonian Wild—200,000 animal pictures*
- *Wiki Images*

Internet privacy websites. If you can't find these by Googling the website, visit Ask a Tech Teacher and the Digital Citizenship resource page:

- *Internet safety video—a day in a digital citizen's life*
- *Net Safety (from Planet Nutshell)*
- *Privacy on the internet*

Steps

Note: Preview the public-domain websites listed above to be sure they fit your particular student group.

____Gather students on the class rug and review last year's discussions on the meaning of 'digital citizens'. Solicit ideas and experiences from students.

____Discuss the potential risks and dangers associated with online communications. Have any students had experience with this through their families?

____Discuss '**netiquette**'—'internet etiquette'—as it relates to second grade. What do they remember from last year?

____What is **cyberbullying**? How is it like and different from bullying on the playground? What does the prefix 'cyber' mean?

____For 15-30 minutes of several weekly lessons, focus discussion on 1) **image copyrights**, and 2) **digital privacy**

_____Discuss what *image copyright* means. Why is it important? How do you identify a copyrighted image? Show students what one looks like.

_____Discuss how students found pictures for a recent research project (for instance, my second graders research life cycles and find images online of the stages in an animal's development).

_____Give students time to visit several websites listed above that offer copyright-free images, like *Photos for Class* or *Smithsonian Wild*.

_____Show students where websites list rights associated with images.

_____In another class period, discuss the concept of **online presence**. This includes when students create a story using Storybird or Animoto (see future lesson)—websites that save the student's story online and make them available to others to read. What does that mean? Is that safe? How can students protect their online privacy? Discuss the importance of never posting private information about themselves online, including their pictures.

_____To support this discussion, create avatars (a fake profile image that looks nothing like the student) using one of these mostly-free web-based avatar creators:

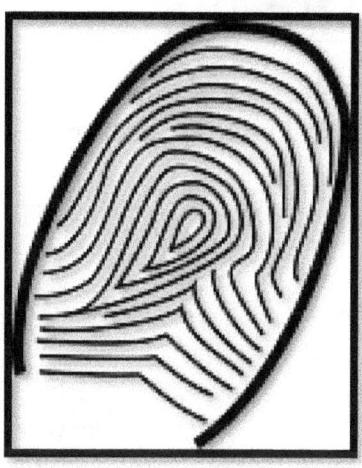

- *Avatar–a monster (from Thirteen.org)*
- *Buddy Poke 3D--students create 3D avatars*
- *DoppelMe*
- *FaceQ–create an avatar (app)*
- *Lego you*
- *Pickaface*
- *Pixton — fee-based*
- *Plotagon (web/iOS/Android) --students star in an animated movie. They pick a scene, add dialogue, add sound effects.*

_____Publish student avatar to the class wiki, blog, or website. Discuss what that means and how it is secure (because of the firewalls on the school's blog, wiki, website).

_____During sponge or free time throughout the year, circle back on these concepts by visiting online websites listed above or others that you like.

Extension:

Research a project that goes to specific websites as a method of teaching safe search methods.

Inquiry-based Teaching with PBL

#3—How to Animoto

Collaborations	OVERVIEW	Troubleshooting
<ul><li>Presenting</li><li>Research</li><li>Speaking/listening</li><li>Writing</li></ul>	Students collaborate on resource-gathering and present the final project with Animoto. Appropriate for grades 2-8	Rendering the video doesn't work. *It takes a while to render. Explain students must be patient.*
Time Required 30 minutes (2 sessions)		**ISTE Standards** 1, 2, 4

Examples of movie-making webtools. If you can't find these by Googling the website, visit Ask a Tech Teacher and the Video resource page:

- *Adobe Spark—free tools to create videos; great for Chromebooks*
- *Animaker*
- *Animoto*
- *Go animate*
- *iMovie*
- *PlayPosit—interactive videos*
- *Spark video — for Chromebooks and iOS; add personal narrative, images. Use a story template or start from scratch*
- *WeVideo—collaborative; record on mobile devices; edit on desktop; great for Chromebooks*

Steps

Note: Check each webtool out before using it to be sure it's appropriate for your student group.

____The goal of this project goal is to build knowledge on a topic and share it in a visually exciting way with friends.

____Students work in groups of two-three to research an inquiry-driven topic that supports a class unit. Each group will collect five-ten images and five-ten facts. Take brief notes (as with PowerPoint, Animoto is not text-intensive), and support text with images.

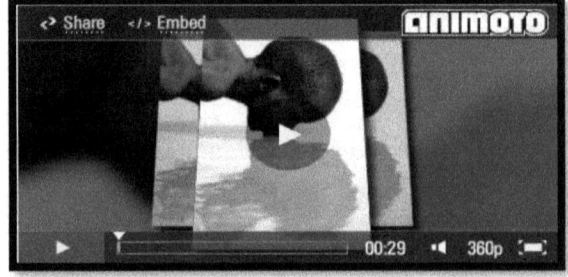

____When all resources are gathered and in the correct order, students are ready to create the Animoto movie.

____Animoto is a movie creator that is simple enough to be student-directed. Make this student-directed rather than teacher directed by watching some of the many great videos that explain the use of Animoto (check YouTube or SqoolTube for ideas) or create one yourself using a free screen recording tool like the native screen recording tool on your Mac, PC, iPad, or Chromebook.

_____As students watch one or more of these videos, be available for questions or problem-solving. *Note: This teach-themselves approach may be more suited to older students or those with experience making videos.*

_____Done? Ask a student to demonstrate. This may be one who has used Animoto in the past. If no one volunteers, you can begin the process but ask for student assistance on each step (*What do we do next? Do you see a tool that says 'add music'?*)

_____Have each student pick a background that fits the topic.

_____Upload one image per slide from those gathered by the group until all images are added. Add explanatory text to the slide or create a new slide with text.

_____Arrange slides to effectively convey the message. Include a title slide, an introductory slide, an 'About the Author' slide, and a summative slide that concludes the presentation.

_____Next, add music that enhances the message. These can be from the webtool's collection or uploaded from the school's collection. Make sure that what students pick from are all public domain music. Help them understand what this means.

_____Now let students try their own. Assist as needed, answer questions, but this is a student-directed project.

_____When they finish, have them watch their project for accuracy. Edit as needed before submitting.

_____Embed Animotos into the class wiki, blog, or website, or to the school website if appropriate. Circle back on the class discussion about 'digital privacy' as you upload to the website. Is this movie secure? Why are you concerned about student privacy?

_____Provide time for students to go through each other's presentations and add comments (if that is possible).

_____When done, ask students to reflect on this exercise. What was difficult, easy? What did they learn? Would they like to do this again?

Extension:

Instead of using Animoto's stock backgrounds, upload one from the school's collection about the topic.

Use PowerPoint to turn a slideshow into a movie. Students will love this because they already know how to use PowerPoint so they don't have to learn anything new.

You can also use the education version of Canva. This may be better suited for olders than 2nd grade.

Inquiry-based Teaching with PBL

#4—Life Cycle Reports

Collaborations	OVERVIEW	Troubleshooting
• Art • Reading • Writing	Use photos to convey a story that words can't. **Appropriate for grades 2-5**	1) Ads distract 2nd graders. If possible, have an ed account. 2) 2nd graders might find folding difficult. Help as needed.
Time Required 30 minutes (2 sessions)		**ISTE Standards** 2, 4

Examples of other digital storytelling webtools. If you can't find these by Googling the website, visit Ask a Tech Teacher and the Digital Storytelling resource page:

- *Adobe Spark Video–digital stories that blend images and audio into a video*
- *Big Huge Labs*
- *Book Creator*
- *Little Bird Tales–upload drawings, add student voice*
- *Shadow Puppet EDU – make videos to tell stories, explain ideas, & document learning (app)*
- *StoryBird—-storytelling with art–beautiful*
- *Storyboard That–use their storytelling layout*

Steps

_____Many webtools are available for digital storytelling (see the list above) to support science inquiry into topics like life cycles. One of the most creative (and free) is Big Huge Labs.

_____Big Huge Labs is an online 'desktop publishing' tool to create posters, mosaics, trading cards, calendars, billboards, jigsaw puzzles and thirty other projects using images. It is particularly suitable to elementary-age students because:

1) *It's easy to use. Most projects require about two steps.*
2) *It challenges students to manipulate photos to convey their message.*
3) *It requires creativity and out-of-the-box thinking—two skills valued in today's educational environment.*

_____The goal of this project is to build knowledge on the topic and then share it in a visually exciting way.

_____Students work in groups of two-three to collect six images (with proper citations) for a life cycle report on the stages in the animal's growth. Or instead of life cycles, use a topic being discussed in your class.

_____Once images are collected, open Big Huge Labs. No log-in is required but images can't be saved to the site's server. If your school has a Big Huge Labs education account, students can create their own account without requiring an email and save formatted photos to the internet for availability from home, in other parts of the school, and on other devices. This feature also has no ads—a wonderful plus with the curiosity of second graders.

_____If this is one of the first times students have done a project online, review internet safety best practices.

_____Tour Big Huge Lab's site layout and the myriad of projects using images.

_____Students will use the Cube for this project. Demonstrate how to use it with the collected images. The Cube works particularly well with a life cycle report where each side is a stage in the animal's growth (with room for a title and a conclusion).

_____Upload six images saved by one of the groups, then print and fold so the student has an animal life cycle cube. Big Huge Labs has an option for adding die numbers to each face which might be a good idea for a life cycle's stages.

_____Now let students try, working in the same groups that collected the photos.

_____This is a student-directed activity, testing their ability to look at the program, make decisions on what must be done next, and remember what you did during the demonstration. You may be surprised how many have no problem accomplishing this project.

_____Once they are printed and folded, the cubes can be hung in the classroom or placed on an open table for viewing.

_____When done, ask students to reflect on this exercise. What was difficult? Easy? What did they learn?

Extension:

Use BHL badges to create name tags for field trips, Trading Cards for Flora and Fauna Cards, an avatar to use with student online presence, a magazine cover for a book read during class, and Movie Posters to share about a time in history. Once created, they can be printed or saved (a screen shot works well in Big Huge Labs, especially if you don't have an account) and published to a class website, wiki, or blog.

Notes

Inquiry-based Teaching with PBL

#5—How to Keyboard in 2nd Grade

Collaborations	OVERVIEW	Troubleshooting
• Communication • Writing	Students continue keyboarding instruction in a fun, age-appropriate way.	Students can't use the right fingers on right keys. *Remind them they don't worry about this until next year.*
Time Required 15 minutes, repeat		**ISTE Standards** 6

Examples of web-based keyboarding tools. If you can't find these by Googling the website, visit Ask a Tech Teacher and the Keyboarding resource page:

- *ABCYa Keyboard challenge*
- *Barracuda game*
- *Dance Mat Typing*
- *Finger jig practice game*
- *Popcorn Typer*
- *Tux Typing*
- *Typaphone—make music while you type*
- *Type Dojo—select by grade level*
- *Typing Tournament*

Steps

____Keyboarding is a cumulative skill. What can be effectively learned in one grade depends heavily upon what is learned in earlier years. If hunt 'n peck habits become ingrained, it becomes difficult to develop keyboarding competence when it matters in later years.

____Discuss why students learn keyboarding. Here are reasons (zoom in if needed to view better):

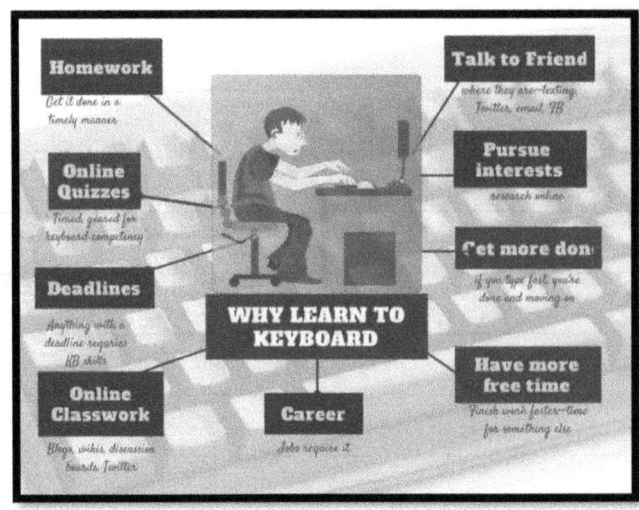

_____If this is the first keyboard class this year, review:

- *Caps lock and shift—what is the difference?*
- *Backspace and delete—what's the difference?*
- *Tab—what's this used for?*
- *Home row—why is it more important than the others?*
- *Top row with numbers*
- *Numeric keypad—for numbers if NumLock invoked*

_____Start with finger warm-ups to show students they have five fingers, all work, some are stronger than others. These are good for youngers:

Warm up Fingers
- Lay your hand flat on a table (in the inset, the book is the table) with fingers touching. Spread fingers apart as far as possible and hold for three seconds. Close fingers. Repeat 10 times.

- Next, lift each finger, move around, then lower it.

Stretch Fingers
- Hold hands facing each other. Touch thumbs. Touch first fingers, and so on. Repeat until all fingers are touching.

- With fingers pressed together, pull palms away creating a cup shape with fingers and palm. Starting at finger tips, slowly move palms closer, rolling the pressure down the fingers until fingers are pressed together. Hold for 10 seconds. Repeat 10 times.

Aerobics for Fingers
- Hold hand in the air with fingers spread like a "high-five." Move thumb to the palm and press. Bring thumb back to starting position and move the first finger to palm and press. Move it back to the starting position and repeat with remaining fingers.

Fingers not pressing into the palm should be held straight. After one round, try again a little faster. Repeat 10 times, increasing speed with each round.

Weight Training for Fingers
- Grab a scrap piece of paper and crumble it into a ball with one hand. Squeeze tightly and hold for 10 seconds. Repeat with the other hand.

_____Students sit at keyboard with proper posture (zoom in to view inset if needed):

- *Sit straight, feet flat, body centered in front of keyboard*
- *Keep elbows close to sides*
- *Keep fingers slightly curved*

- *Play keyboard like a piano (or violin, guitar, recorder). Don't use pointer for all keys*
- *Fingers move, not hands. Hands stay anchored to f and j keys*

____Using Dance Mat Typing, Popcorn Typer, or Type Dojo, work on one row at a time for ten minutes per class, starting with home row. When comfortable with key placement, have students cover their hands with a cloth. They love this—see it as a badge of honor to type with hands hidden. Don't worry if they don't reach this level in 2nd grade. It'll come.

____By end of Month #1, home row is memorized and students are ready for QWERTY row. By end of Month #2, move on to lower row.

____By Month #4, use software like Type to Learn or a free year-long online keyboarding program like Typing Web or TuxTyping. Rotate programs throughout the year so students don't get tired of one.

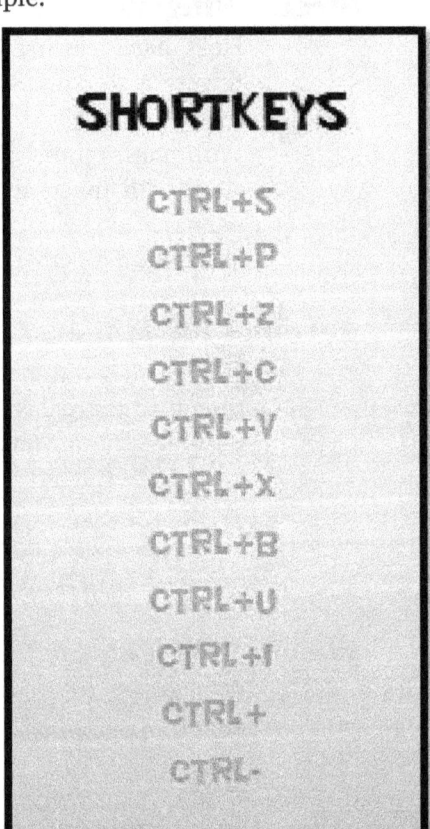

____Remind students they have eight fingers and two thumbs—not just two pointers that hunt and peck.

____During class typing time, walk around and make sure students follow good posture.

____Consistently throughout the year, introduce and reinforce the use of keyboard shortcuts. These are quick two-key macros that accomplish commonly-performed tasks. For example:

- *When saving, have students Ctrl+S*
- *When printing, have students Ctrl+P*
- *When exiting a program, Alt+F4*
- *When copying something, Ctrl+C*
- *When pasting something, Ctrl+V (why not Ctrl+P?)*

Students love to show off their techie-ness by using these and teaching them to others. See inset for favorites.

____Occasionally through the year, have students use a program like TypingTest.com (or similar) to get used to the upper grade concept of speed and accuracy. There is no speed and accuracy goal in second grade. The only goal is to think about those concepts.

____Keep keyboarding fun as students develop good habits. They'll need these when speed and accuracy become important.

Extension:

Every time something can be performed with a shortkey, ask students who knows the shortkey for that function. For example, when inserting the date, ask who knows what the shortkey for that function is.

Any time students type, remind them that's the right time to focus on correct posture and hand position—nut just during keyboard time practice time.

Third Grade

#1—Compare With Venn Diagrams

Collaborations	OVERVIEW	Troubleshooting
• History • Language arts • Math	Compare and contrast two cultures studied in class *Appropriate for grades 3-6 with some modification*	1) Bullets don't work in text boxes. Push Alt+0149—with number pad 2) The pictures are too dark—I can't see the text. Adjust transparency.
Time Required 40 minutes		**ISTE Standards** 2, 4, 6

Examples of webtools for Venn Diagrams. If you can't find these by Googling the website, visit Ask a Tech Teacher and the Visual Learning resource page:

- *Canva (for Education)*
- *Google Draw*
- *MS Word or Google Docs*
- *MS Publisher*
- *ReadWriteThink*
- *Storyboard That!*

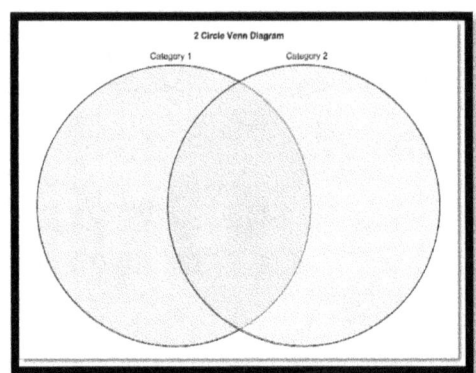

Steps

_____A **Venn Diagram** is a graphic organizer that visually compares/contrasts concepts. They are great for visual learners and fun for all students.

_____In this case, we'll use Venn Diagrams to better understand the similarities and differences between the Egyptian and Navajo cultures (pick topics that work for your class).

_____Draw two overlapping circles on the class screen. Label each with the cultures to be compared. Ask two students to come up and write down characteristics of each culture, in the correct circle, as students come up with them. Encourage students with organic questions that jog their memory about what they read in textbooks, discussed in class, saw in videos, or learned through other classroom resources.

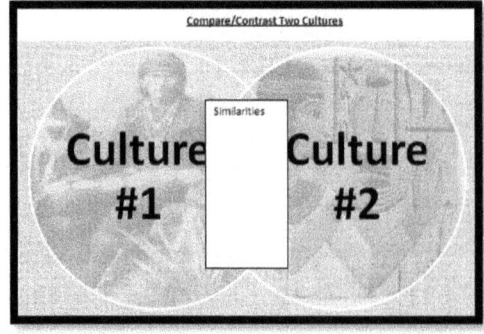

_____When all characteristics are listed, ask the students to sit down and invite different students to identify which characteristics are in both lists and ask the student to write it in the overlapping portion of the circles.

_____Students have now created a Venn Diagram.

____Open MS Word or another Venn Diagram tool from the list above. Add heading (name, teacher, date) at the top.

____Insert a SmartArt Venn Diagram. Delete one of the circles so there are just two that overlap.

____Have students copy the characteristics from the class screen for each culture.

____Add a text box to the center of the two circles (see inset). In here, add the similarities between the two cultures.

____Take a screen shot and save to class wiki, blog, or website (if available).

____When done, ask students to reflect on this exercise. What was difficult, easy? What did they learn? Did they find it easier to understand the two cultures by listing their characteristics in this manner?

Extension:

Add a background to each circle which is a picture of the culture being characterized in that circle (see inset).

Use a Venn Diagram with three circles to compare/contrast three cultures. Explain the parts of the three overlapping circles: All sets and subsets of the groups are displayed visually using the overlapping circles and their parts. This is a good introduction to set theory for older students.

Notes

Inquiry-based Teaching with PBL

#2—Puzzle Maker to Prepare for Tests

Collaborations	OVERVIEW	Troubleshooting
• Critical thinking • Problem solving • Reading • Writing	Use a Puzzle Maker to reinforce classroom concepts *Appropriate for grades 3-6*	One of the puzzles doesn't come up on our browser. Try a different browser.
Time Required 30 minutes (2 sessions)		**ISTE Standards** 1, 3, 4

Examples of study guides using puzzle webtools. If you can't find these by Googling the website, visit Ask a Tech Teacher and the Study Guides resource page:

- *ClassTools Arcade Game*
- *Crossword Puzzle Generator*
- *Discovery's PuzzleMaker*
- *Wolfram Alpha's Widget Creator*—*lots of flexibility, but geared for embedding into websites rather than simple sharing*
- *WordSearch*—*print, do online, hover over word for definition*

Steps

___Have students create their own study guides or formative assessments. They'll come up with the facts they consider important (you might be surprised by their take-away from your lessons), have fun testing each other, and learn a lot by peer-teaching.

___Let students know that they will prepare their own study guides during the unit or at the end of the unit. Have them highlight the information throughout the unit they feel is particularly important as it is presented. This way, by the time they must prepare the assessment or study guide, they are ready.

___There are several puzzle generators that work for this project (see the options above). Let students experiment with all.

___Have students select the puzzle maker they want to use. Let's say they selected *Discovery's PuzzleMaker*. This is a good choice because it provides many options for the creation of the puzzle—WordSearch, Crisscross, Mazes, Math Squares, Cryptograms, Hidden Message, and more.

___Students work in groups for both the selection and the implementation of this project.

___Provide sufficient time for students to write down 2 or 3 questions based on the material learned in the unit. These can be derived from classroom discussion, notes, textbooks, and/or other.

- 54 -

_____Demonstrate how to create a puzzle on the class screen. Encourage students to assist. Prompt them with questions about what is next.

_____Once the demo is complete, let students loose. Creating a puzzle is student-directed but assist if they get stuck.

_____Save and upload to the class website, blog, or wiki to share.

_____Give students time to share their study guide with others in the class to see who gets the right answers.

_____When done, ask them to reflect on this exercise. What did they learn? Did they learn more this way than other ways of studying?

_____This type of student-generated assessment has the advantage that you as the teacher get a good idea about areas the students are having problems with by looking at the questions asked and not asked.

Extension:

Once the puzzles are created, have a contest to see who gets the most right answers on the most puzzles. Have each student MC their own puzzle, pass them out, collect and grade answers.

This may be used as the assessment for the unit.

Notes

#3—Create a Timeline of Events

Collaborations	OVERVIEW	Troubleshooting
• Listening • Reading • Speaking • Writing	Students create a timeline of events using text, visual, audio. *Appropriate for grades 3-6 with some adaptations*	We have nowhere to embed the timeline *Take a screen shot and upload to class website.*
Time Required 30 minutes (2 sessions)		**ISTE Standards** 1, 3, 4, 6

Examples of timeline webtools. If you can't find these by Googling the website, visit Ask a Tech Teacher and the Visual Learning-Timelines resource page:

- *Excel—instructions on Eric Curts*
- *PowerPoint—instructions on FreeTech4Teachers*
- *Read-Write-Think Timeline*
- *Storyboard That—use their timeline layout*
- *Sutori*

Steps

_____Pre-sell project by creating a class timeline on a book being read, a history chapter, or class events (like holidays, birthdays, field trips—the inclusions are endless). Post it to the class wiki, website, blog, or on the wall. Update it daily. It won't be long before students are checking to see what has been added, making their own suggestions, eager to create their own.

_____Students work with a partner to research a topic. Gather ten sequential dates of events with several sentences explaining the importance of each date. Include one image, audio, or video for each date. Keep a list of sources. Research sites include encyclopedias, newspapers, internet websites, magazines, and more.

_____Timelines will be created using a free web-based tool like those listed above or one you prefer. Some require an online account and most are free. Preview those listed to see which is best suited to your student group.

_____Share timelines created by prior students so current students get a better understanding of expectations.

_____Create a sample timeline so students can see how it works.

_____Have each student or group of students create a timeline with ten events and ten images/videos, using appropriate facts and descriptive details to support main ideas or themes. Drag each event to its correct temporal order.

_____Check grammar and spelling, and sentence fluency. Be sure the main ideas are clear and well developed. All facts should be accurate and appropriate. Detail should be descriptive. Media should reinforce text, and both text and images should convey the same message. As a whole, all forms of media should enhance the development of the central ideas or themes

_____Before submitting, have students watch each other's project to see if the message is clear. If feedback indicates changes are required, students can edit, add more pictures, audio or text to better convey their message.

_____When the timeline is completed, use the embed code (if available) or a screenshot to publish it to the class blog, wiki, or website.

_____Have students/groups present their timelines using the class screen. Drill down to videos and/or links to provide detail for dates and events. Speak clearly, at a pace that is easily understood, and a volume that can be heard throughout the room.

_____At the end, ask students to reflect on this exercise. Did they learn more by presenting their information this way than other ways?

Extension:

Have students collect all events in a history unit being studied. Post to class screen as a list and have students create a timeline showing their temporal location.

Create a timeline that extends around the wall of the classroom. This could be units you're studying in history or schoolyear events.

Notes

Inquiry-based Teaching with PBL

#4—How to Survive on Landforms

Collaborations	OVERVIEW	Troubleshooting
• Reading • Speaking/listening • Writing	*Students learn about landforms by researching how to survive if stranded on them.* *Appropriate for grades 3, 4*	Some links won't open. *Is Flash up to date? Check with IT to see if there's an infrastructure reason. Try a different browser or reboot the computer.*
Time Required 25 minutes (repeat)		**ISTE Standards** 3, 4

Examples of websites where you can find information about surviving landforms and natural disasters:

- *Discovery Channel*
- *History Channel*
- *How Stuff Works*
- *National Geographic*

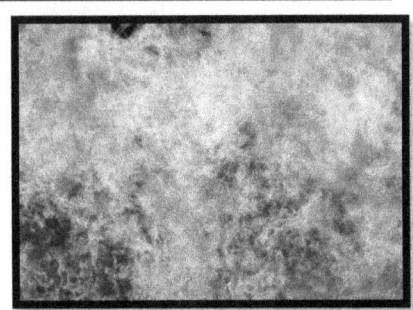

Steps

____If you want to spice up a unit on landforms, have students investigate surviving natural habitats. To do so, they must understand the flora and fauna, dangers, climate, natural habitat, predators/prey, fear as a survival strategy, and helpers.

____Assign landforms by student/groups. Include rivers, rainforests, jungle, mountains, prairie, African savanna, oceans, mountains, snowstorms, hypothermia in water, floods, a shipwreck, the woods, or any other natural disaster or natural habitat.

____As they view websites, have them collect information on how to 1) find food, 2) find water, 3) find shelter, 4) avoid predators, 5) find clothing, 6) alert rescuers of their location, and 7) find protection from the elements

____Have students share how they would survive on the landform they chose. Cover all questions included in the research.

____When done, ask them to reflect on this exercise. What was difficult, easy? What did they learn? How does this approach to learning compare to other methodology used in class?

Inquiry-based Teaching with PBL

#5—How To Avoid Cyberbullying

Collaborations	OVERVIEW	Troubleshooting
• Presenting • Reading • Speaking/listening • Writing	*Why is it important to be a good digital citizenship? How can students do this?* ***Appropriate for 3-8 with adaptations***	*We don't have blogs No worries. Create a wiki page in the class wiki that can be used as a discussion forum. Have students add their thoughts here and comment on the thoughts of others.*
Time Required 30 minutes, repeat		**ISTE Standards** 5

Examples of cyberbully resources. If you can't find these by Googling them, visit Ask a Tech Teacher and the Digital Citizenship-Cyberbullying resource page:

- *Bullied to Death--a true story of a teen who commit suicide over cyberbullying*
- *Calling my Childhood Bully—a video where a boy who has been videoed calls the boy who did it when they have both grown up (7 min.)*
- *Cyberbully—90-minute movie*
- *Cyberbullying—You're not Alone — Hector's World*
- *Cyberbullying--geared for fifth grade and up; it includes the common questions students may ask and provides the answers*
- *Cyberbullying—BrainPop*
- *Cyberbullying—what is it*
- *Think Time: How Does Cyberbullying Affect You--a short video that hits all the important points of cyberbullying*
- *What is Cyberbullying? from Commonsense Media*

Note: Preview these websites before showing them to students. Some are graphic and may not be appropriate for your student group.

Steps

_____Review last year's discussions on the meaning of '**digital citizens**', 'digital privacy' and 'image copyrights'. Solicit ideas and experiences from students.

_____Discuss '**plagiarism**'. What does it mean? Why should you give credit to original authors of information? What are the consequences of NOT doing that?

_____Discuss the potential risks and dangers associated with online communications.

_____What is '**netiquette**'? Discuss 'internet etiquette' as it relates to a third grader. What do students remember about netiquette from prior discussions?

_____What is **cyberbullying**? Do any students know someone who's been bullied? Or cyberbullied? Why is that bad? What does the prefix 'cyber' mean? How could you bully someone online? Is that OK because no one knows it was you?

_____Why do we start this topic in 3rd grade? Because already, 3rd graders are being cyberbullied. As you work through this lesson plan, adapt it to your student group. But, make sure you cover this topic.

_____Cyberbullying is when someone is taunted physically or mentally by others via the internet. Wikipedia defines "cyberbullying" as:

the use of information technology to repeatedly harm or harass other people in a deliberate manner

_____Explain that cyberbullying is no longer relegated to the playground or the neighborhood. It now regularly happens in the cyberworld. Kids don't expect that and often don't know how to handle it.

_____In October 2006, thirteen-year-old Megan Meier hung herself in her bedroom closet after suffering months of cyberbullying. She believed her tormentors' horrid insults, never thought she could find a way to stop them and killed herself. She's not the only one. In fact, according to StopBullying.gov, 52 percent of young people report being cyberbullied and over half of them don't report it to their parents.

_____Cyberbullying occurs on not just social media like Twitter, Facebook, and topical forums—places most parents and kids think are domains of teens—but on multiplayer games and school discussion boards. Examples include mean texts or emails, insulting snapchats, rumors posted on social networking sites, and embarrassing photos or videos.

_____How serious is it? *The National Youth Violence Prevention Resource Center* estimates that nearly 30 percent of American youth are either a bully or a target of bullying. 7% of high school students commit suicide, some because of cyberbullying:

On October 7, 2003, Ryan Halligan committed suicide by hanging himself [after being cyberbullied by high school classmates]. His body was found later by his older sister.

_____It gets worse every year as the Internet plays an increasingly dominant part in student lives at home and school. Exponentially worse. Because this crime is hidden in the vastness of the world wide web, the bully considers themselves anonymous, hiding behind their handles and fake profiles, making it difficult to find the guilty parties. As a result, too often, everyone thinks someone else is responsible for stopping it. Parents think they're invading their child's privacy by monitoring social media accounts and teachers think they don't have enough time to monitor school-related virtual meeting places. What makes it even harder to identify and less likely to solve is that students often are reluctant to ask for help.

_____Effects of Cyberbullying:

- Kids who are cyberbullied are more likely to:
    - *use alcohol and drugs*
    - *skip school*
    - *experience in-person bullying*
    - *be unwilling to attend school*
    - *receive poor grades*
    - *have lower self-esteem*
    - *have more health problems*

_____Projects related to cyberbullying include:

- Have students model with a friend how they would respond to a cyberbully. They can pick the method or you can suggest one appropriate to 3rd grade.
- Discuss how students would react to being cyberbullied? How would they help a friend? Should they help a friend? When is it right to find an adult to help?
- Have students sit in groups and discuss their thoughts on the movie they watched. Then, bring the group together and discuss as a class.
- Have students create a comic (using a comic creator they are familiar with) showing a student being bullied online and how s/he deals with it. Use information gained from videos watched during class. Walk around to help students focus in on the right age-appropriate response.
- Have student groups brainstorm cyberbullying. Visually represent thoughts with a mindmap.
- Have students create a Voki sharing how s/he was cyberbullied and what s/he did about it. This would include an avatar who talks about the subject.
- Have students create a blog post (if your third graders are blogging in class) explaining what they know about being a digital citizen. How does being a good digital citizen address cyberbullying? Visit the posts of classmates. Contribute comments. Good comments include a compliment, suggestion, and/or question. And, don't forget to use best writing skills.

_____Discuss this topic with your students every year, starting as soon as they use multi-player games (often as young as second grade). You think they're OK because you disabled the online access — think again. These clever digital natives take figuring out how to circumvent your protections as a challenge. Once the emotional damage is done, it's difficult to undo.

Fourth Grade

#1—How do I Keyboard in 4th Grade?

Collaborations	OVERVIEW	Troubleshooting
• Internetting • Researching • Writing	*Develop touch typing to build on skills learned in K-3. Good habits+Accuracy+Practice=Speed*	I can't type with hands covered. *Keep practicing.*

Time Required	ISTE Standards
15 minutes (repeat throughout year)	5

Examples of keyboarding webtools. If you can't find these by Googling the website, visit Ask a Tech Teacher and the Keyboarding resource page:

- *ABCYa--Keyboard challenge*
- *Dance Mat Typing*
- *GoodTyping.com*
- *KAZ--speed typing in 90 minutes*
- *Keyboard practice—quick start*
- *Keyboarding—more lessons*
- *Popcorn Typer*
- *QwertyTown—fee-based, well done*
- *Typaphone--make music while you type*
- *TypeDojo -- word lists, 10-key, and more*
- *Type Kids—graduated program*
- *Typing.com*
- *TypingArena--lots of games*
- *Typing Tournament*
- *Typing.IO--typing code for practice*

Steps

____Keyboarding is a cumulative skill – what can be effectively learned in fourth grade depends heavily upon what has been learned in prior years. If hunt 'n peck habits become ingrained, it's difficult to develop competency in keyboarding skills.

____Basics to be focused on during fourth grade are:

- *Correct keying technique*
- *Start hands on home row*
- *Correct reaches to all keys*
- *Correct posture*

- Sit up straight, shoulders back, head up, body centered in front of keyboard
- Elbows close to sides
- Fingers slightly curved

- *Copy to the left or right of keyboard, eyes on copy or screen—NOT keyboard*
- *Key with a steady even pace, eyes on screen, keys memorized*
- Use keyboard shortcuts (i.e., Ctrl+B, Shift+Alt+D)
- Apply keyboarding skills whenever possible, not just during typing practice

____Start each quarter/semester with a keyboard quiz to determine student speed and accuracy. As students take their speed quiz, I anecdotally notice who uses all fingers. Those that aren't lose points.

____The first quiz is the benchmark. The rest are graded based on improvement:

- *20% improvement*   10/10
- *10-20% improvement*   9/10
- *1-10% improvement*   8/10
- *No improvement*   7/10
- *Slowed down*   6/10

____Students who reach the grade level standard for speed and accuracy get a free dress pass (we are a uniform school). This is exciting for them.

____Grade level standards are:

3rd Grade:	*15 wpm*
4th Grade:	*25 wpm*
5th Grade:	*30 wpm*
6th Grade:	*35 wpm*

____Students work in pairs to fill in all key names. They must retake until they pass. This works—I often see students who didn't pass memorizing key placement so they can get through the quiz the next time. This knowledge of key placement quickly translates to improved speed and accuracy.

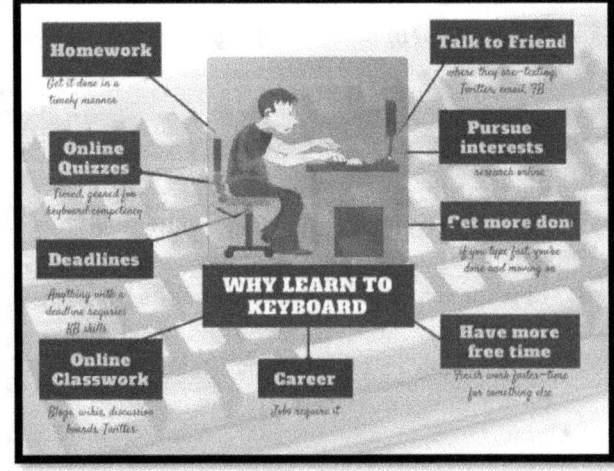

____Students work on one row of the keyboard per month: 1) first month, home row, 2) second, QWERTY row, 3) finally, lower row. Students practice 10-15 minutes during class time and 45 minutes per week as homework.

____Students practice using a keyboard practice program like Dance Mat Typing or Popcorn Typer that works on one row at a time.

____After three months (when all three rows are completed), student switch to a graduated program like Type to Learn or Typing Web (free). By this time, students must cover their hands while practicing. I provide cloths they can use at school and home.

____The focus is now on memorizing keys. Once they know key placement, speed and accuracy will come. It feels hard at first and quickly becomes easier.

____Several times a month, do finger warm-ups. These show students that they have five working fingers, and that some are stronger than others. Remind students they have eight fingers and two thumbs—not just two pointers that hunt and peck.

Warm up Fingers

- Lay your hand flat on a table (in the inset, the book is the table) with fingers touching. Spread fingers apart as far as possible and hold for three seconds. Close fingers. Repeat 10 times.

- Next, lift each finger, move around, then lower it.

Stretch Fingers

- Hold hands facing each other. Touch thumbs. Touch first fingers, and so on. Repeat until all fingers are touching.

- With fingers pressed together, pull palms away creating a cup shape with fingers and palm. Starting at finger tips, slowly move palms closer, rolling the pressure down the fingers until fingers are pressed together. Hold for 10 seconds. Repeat 10 times.

Aerobics for Fingers

- Hold hand in the air with fingers spread like a "high-five." Move thumb to the palm and press. Bring thumb back to starting position and move the first finger to palm and press. Move it back to the starting position and repeat with remaining fingers.

Fingers not pressing into the palm should be held straight. After one round, try again a little faster. Repeat 10 times, increasing speed with each round.

Weight Training for Fingers

- Grab a scrap piece of paper and crumble it into a ball with one hand. Squeeze the paper ball tightly and hold for 10 seconds. Repeat with the other hand.

____Start each quarter/semester with a blank keyboard quiz.

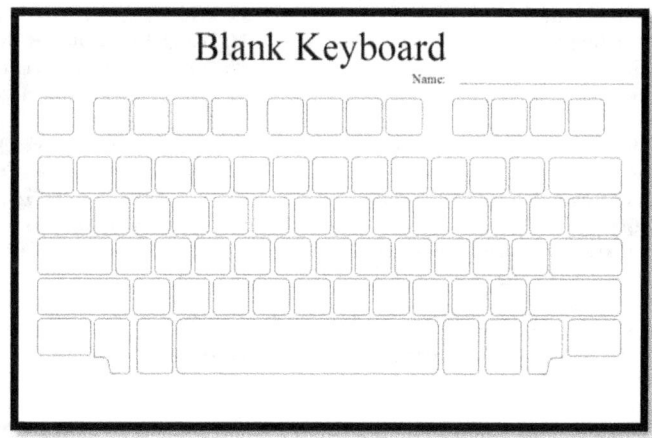

_____Consistently throughout the year, introduce and reinforce the use of keyboard shortcuts (see earlier lessons for age-appropriate shortkeys). These are quick two- or three-key macros that accomplish commonly-performed tasks. Students love these and like to show off their techie-ness by using them and teaching them to others. See inset for two favorites.

_____Occasionally through the year, have students use a program called TypingTest.com to test their speed and accuracy.

_____Keep keyboarding fun, but make sure students develop good habits.

Extension:

At the end of the year, have a Team Challenge. Break the class into teams of five. Ask a question from the list and give only three seconds to answer. They can answer verbally or with the correct finger. The focus is on speed—students must know the answers, not have to think about it. Here's a sample of questions you might include (zoom in if needed):

ANNUAL TEAM CHALLENGE—KEYBOARD

Review

Review the following concepts. These are similar to questions that will be asked during the upcoming Team Challenge to find the summer's most tech-savvy student!

1. What's the computer log in
2. What's the computer password
3. What's your password for TTL4
4. What row do your finger start on before you even type a letter
5. What's the row above home row
6. What's the row below home row called
7. How do you find the f and j key without looking
8. Name three keys you use your pinkie to push
9. Name three keys you use your ring finger to push
10. Name three keys you use your middle finger to push
11. Name three keys you use your pointer to push
12. Name one key you use your right thumb to push
13. Which finger do you use for the backspace key
14. Which finger do you use for the shift key
15. Which finger do you use for the enter key
16. Which finger do you use for the escape key
17. What are three rules of how you sit at the keyboard
18. Do you have cat's paws or dog paws at the computer
19. Why (do you use cat's paws or dog paws)
20. What part of the chair do you sit on when keyboarding
21. Where are your elbows when keyboarding
22. Where does your right thumb rest when keyboarding
23. What is typing without looking at the keys called
24. Which finger pushes the a key
25. Which finger pushes the b key
26. Which finger pushes the ac key
27. Which finger pushes the d key
28. Which finger pushes the e key
29. Which finger pushes the f key
30. Which finger pushes the g key
31. Which finger pushes the h key
32. Which finger pushes the i key
33. Which finger pushes the j key
34. Which finger pushes the k key
35. What finger pushes enter
36. What's the keyboard shortcut to exit a program
37. As a general rule, which finger pushes a key
38. How do you capitalize a letter
39. As a general rule, do you fingers move or your hands in finding the keys
40. What is one keyboard shortcut
41. What is a desktop

#2—What is Digital Citizenship?

Collaborations	OVERVIEW	Troubleshooting
• Reading • Speaking/listening • Writing	Why is it important to be a good digital citizenship? How can students do this?	This frightens some students. *Take extra time to reassure them but reinforce the message.*
Time Required 40 minutes (several sessions)		**ISTE Standards** 5

Examples of Digital Citizenship websites—visit Ask a Tech Teascher's 'Digital Citizenship' resource page and pick the topic you're discussing with students.

Steps

_____Consider this definition of digital citizenship?

> *"...the ability to use technology safely, responsibly, critically, and pro-actively to contribute to society." —California School Library Association, 2011.*

_____Dissect what it means to *'use technology safely, responsibly, critically, and pro-actively to contribute to society'* means. Do students agree?

_____Reflect on how students used to research with libraries, classroom books. Now, it's done online.

_____Review last year's digital citizenship discussion. Solicit ideas and experiences from students.

_____Review these characteristics of a digital citizen:

- Respect privacy and freedom of speech.
- Use internet confidently and capably.
- Use and develop critical thinking skills.
- Use it to participate in educational and cultural activities.
- Use it to relate to others in positive, meaningful ways.
- Actively promote digital citizenship values.

> **Digital Citizenship Project**
> *Create a quiz on all aspects of Digital Citizenship using puzzle widgets like (Google the name):*
> - Crossword Puzzle Generator
> - PuzzleMaker by Discovery
> - ClassTools Arcade Game

_____Circle back on these concepts throughout the school year.

Digital Rights and Responsibilities

_____What are the **digital rights and responsibilities** of a fourth grader? Discuss these concepts:

- *Act the same online as you'd act in your neighborhood.*
- *Don't share personal information. Don't ask others for theirs.*
- *Be aware of your surroundings. Know where you are in cyberspace. Act accordingly.*
- *Always show your best side online. As in your community, be kind to others; they return it.*
- *Anonymity doesn't protect the individual. They are easily found with an IP address.*
- *Share knowledge online.*
- *If someone is 'flaming', stop it if possible or leave.*

> **Digital R&R Project**
> *Create a Tagxedo with words that share the digital rights and responsibilities of a fourth grader*

_____Have the class define 'digital rights and responsibilities' like: *Privileges and freedoms extended to digital technology users and behavioral expectations that come with them. Students who use the internet are expected to do so ethically and bear a responsibility to keep it a safe, healthy environment for everyone.*

Cyberbullying

_____What is **cyberbullying**? What does 'cyber' mean? What is the same/different about bullying and cyberbullying? Do students know someone (cyber)bullied?
_____Use tools employed to deal with neighborhood bullies on cyberbullies.
_____Watch these videos (Google for website or find them in Ask a Tech Teacher's digital citizenship resource page):

> **Cyberbullying Project**
> *Have student groups brainstorm cyberbullying. Visually represent thoughts with a mindmap*

- *Common Sense—cyberbullying*
- *Pacer Kids Against Bullying--Six videos from kids like you*

_____Based on what 4th graders understand about digital rights and responsibilities, what is their mandate if they find out someone is being cyberbullied?

Netiquette

_____What is '**netiquette**' to a fourth grader?
_____Basics to discuss:

- *Don't pretend to be someone else online.*
- *Don't post or distribute illegal material.*
- *Don't use abusive or threatening language.*
- *Don't post remarks on sex, race, gender.*
- *Don't obtain or use someone's password.*
- *Don't obtain personal info about someone.*

> **Netiquette Project**
> *Post a Padlet on the class Internet Start Page and have students add a 'note' about what netiquette means to digital citizens.*

_____Here are *Net-Lingo* abbreviations used to communicate:

- **BTW**—*By the way*

- **FWIW**—For what it's worth
- **IMHO**—In my humble opinion
- **OTOH**—On the other hand
- **LOL**—Laughing out loud
- **HHOK**—Ha ha, only kidding
- **YHGTBK**—You have got to be kidding
- **ROTFL**—Rolling on the floor laughing
- **RTM** — Read the manual
- **AMF** — Adios, my friend

_____Discuss email etiquette with students. Review these rules:

- Use proper formatting, spelling, grammar.
- CC anyone you mention.
- Subject line is what your email discusses.
- Answer swiftly; re-read email before sending.
- Don't use capitals—THIS IS SHOUTING.
- Don't leave out the subject line.
- Don't attach unnecessary files.
- Don't overuse high priority.
- Don't email confidential information.
- Don't email offensive remarks.
- Don't forward chain letters.
- Don't open attachments from strangers.

Netiquette Rules
- Be human
- Follow the same rules of behavior you follow in real life
- Be aware of your digital footprint
- Share your knowledge
- Help keep 'flame wars' under control
- Respect other's privacy
- Be forgiving of other's mistakes

EMAIL ETIQUETTE
1. Use proper formatting, spelling, grammar
2. CC anyone you mention
3. Subject line is what your email discusses
4. Answer swiftly
5. Re-read email before sending
6. Don't use capitals—THIS IS SHOUTING
7. Don't leave out the subject line
8. Don't attach unnecessary files
9. Don't overuse high priority
10. Don't email confidential information
11. Don't email offensive remarks
12. Don't forward chain letters or spam
13. Don't open attachments from strangers

_____Discuss safe use of digital communication devices. Do students get distracted by phones? While texting?
_____Three rules students should consider when using a cell phone:

- If you speak loudly, others hear you.
- Don't share private conversations.
- Be aware of your surroundings as you're chatting.

_____Circle back on these concepts throughout the school year.

Digital Privacy

_____Talk about **Digital Privacy**.
_____Discuss how **passwords** protect privacy. Remind students they never share passwords, even with friends.
_____Discuss password guidelines.

Digital Privacy Project
Create an avatar to use as the profile picture on student blog.

Digital Footprint

_____What is a **digital footprint**? Consider this definition:

A digital footprint is the amount of content, whether words, photographs, audio, or video, that is traceable to a given individual. It includes uploaded photographs, blog posts, video files, posts you wrote by friends. Two things are notable - first, it can be permanent; second, more and more of us actively search out digital footprints of peers and are influenced by what we find.
(Education.com)

> **Digital Footprint Project**
> Have students search their name online. What do they find? Put all locations into a Tagxedo shaped like a footprint. Can't find any? Leave the footprint barren. Compare this to digital footprints of student's parents. When done, print and share.

_____Discuss. Why is it important? Reiterate the last phrase--that we are influenced by what we find on a digital footprint.

Plagiarism

_____What does '**plagiarism**' mean? How does it tie into research? Why should students give credit to original authors/artists? What are the consequences?

_____Discuss concepts like:

- image copyrights
- fair use
- public domain

> **Plagiarism Project**
> Create **Voki avatars that discuss the differences between the areas of digital law**. Place Vokis on student blog pages (if students have these) or the class wiki.

_____How does this tie into **Digital Commerce**? What is that?

_____Circle back on these concepts every time students use online resources. You may want to watch these additional resources:

_____Reinforce these concepts by circling back on them every time students go online.

Notes

_____
_____
_____
_____
_____
_____
_____
_____

#3—Classify Animals Like a Pro

Collaborations	OVERVIEW	Troubleshooting
• Critical thinking • History (or other) • Researching • Science	Use a graphic organizer to visually organize animal classifications *Appropriate for Grades 4-6*	There are no thumbnails. No problem. Review how to resize images to fit in the bubble.
Time Required 30 minutes		**ISTE Standards** 2, 4, 6

Examples of graphic organizer webtools . If you can't find these by Googling the website, visit Ask a Tech Teacher and the Graphic Organizer resource page:

- *Education Oasis Graphic Organizers*
- *Eduplace Graphic Organizers*
- *Enchanted Learning Graphic organizers*
- *Holt Graphic organizers*
- *Scholastic Graphic Organizers*
- *Teacher Visio Graphic organizers*

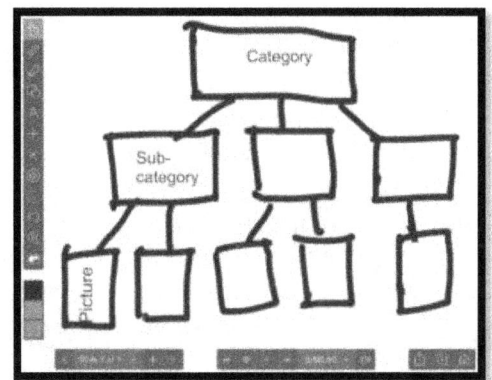

Steps

_____An important competency for all learners is to be able to organize thinking, make connections, and draw conclusions based on available information.

_____One way to accomplish that is with graphic organizers—two-dimensional visual arrays that show relationships among concepts. Graphic organizers sort information to be learned, connect it to what is known, and allow the reader to interact with the text.

_____Why are they effective? It's got to do with the human brain and its natural inclination to arrange information in categories. This approach is particularly helpful in breaking down text when students are reading new or complicated material.

_____This lesson mixes visual with written learning strategies, supporting different learning styles.

_____Demonstrate how a graphic organizer works on the class screen by having students suggest adaptations that have allowed animals to survive environmental changes. Add the framework; add the bubbles and link them as needed.

_____Students work in pairs (or groups) to come up with six animal adaptations and find pictures of them on the internet (remind students to pay attention to copyright protections on images as discussed in other lessons). Encourage them to think back to class discussions, independent research, and information in textbooks as they gather data.

_____ Allow ample time for students to enjoy the plethora of amazing animal pictures that represent the selected adaptations.

_____ Open your graphic organizer program. This could be MS Word, Google Draw, Popplet (for iPads), Bubbl.us, or another option of your choice. Add a heading at the top (name, teacher, date using Shift+Alt+D shortkey). Explain the importance of a heading on every document.

_____ Insert an organizer diagram from one of the collections listed earlier in this lesson. It might look like one of the insets in this lesson.

_____ Add 'Animal Adaptations' as the first tier.

_____ Add the six adaptations that each student group came up with as the second tier.

_____ Add a bubble under the adaptation. Use Google images to find a picture that visually represents each adaptation. I suggest using the thumbnail for this bubble—it fits perfectly and saves a lot of resizing. Plus, it provides a link to information for future research

_____ Save. Publish to class wiki, blog, or website, or have students upload to their own blogs.

_____ Overall, this is a popular project easily completed in 30 minutes.

_____ When done, ask students to reflect on this exercise. What did they learn? Could they visualize the variety of adaptations more easily with this approach than other methods?

Notes

_____

_____

_____

_____

_____

_____

_____

#4—Book Reviews by the Characters

Collaborations	OVERVIEW	Troubleshooting
• Literature • Reading • Speaking/listening • Writing	*Have a book's character explain the who-what-when-where-why-how details.* ***Appropriate for grades 2-5 with some adaptations***	We don't have microphones. *Students can type their dialogue into the Voki and publish it that way.*
Time Required 30 minutes (several sessions)		**ISTE Standards** 2, 3, 4, 5

Examples of audio webtools available for a book review. If you can't find these by Googling the website, visit Ask a Tech Teacher and the Audio resource page:

- *Vocaroo*
- *Voice Thread*
- *Voki*

Steps

____Working in pairs, have students select one character from the book they are currently reading in class (i.e., *Sara Plain and Tall*) until all characters are chosen.

____As students read the book, discuss the critical details of *who, what, when, where, why, and how* (if you have your own favorite characteristics, use those instead). Ask groups to take note of these as they read the book, focusing on their particular character. Additionally, ask them to consider the impact of *plot, setting, action, conclusions, and pacing on their character*.

____When the story is completed, introduce students to a web-based communication tool called Voki—a free service that lets students create interactive avatars, add a voice that says whatever they program it to, and publish the Voki to blogs, wikis or websites (with the education option). If you don't want to use Voki, choose one of the other options listed above or one you are familiar with for this purpose.

____Share examples of Vokis from last year's class and how they can be used to tell important details of a story.

____Voki requires no log-in or password, but you may choose to set up a class account so you can collect student projects. Demonstrate how to create a Voki and program it to speak.

____Have students create a Voki of their character. Customize it as closely as possible to the character in the story including cultural details, accessories, and bling that enhances certain facts and/or details. You may have two students share the same character.

_____Add a background that fits the story setting. This can be selected from what's offered on the website or uploaded from one on the student computer.

_____Next, students write a script for their Voki to speak. Include details like who s/he is, what her/his part is in the story, when and where this occurs, why s/he is important to the story's plot, how the story starts, what problems occur that the character must solve, how s/he arrives at the solution, how all the pieces are tied together at the story's end.

_____Pick a voice that fits the character. Text may be recorded directly into the Voki, typed into the screen, or uploaded from a pre-recorded audio file. Start over if necessary. Concentrate on fluid reading with an understandable pace—not too fast or slow.

_____When completed, have students peer review each other's Vokis.

_____Once Vokis are available online, have students play through all characters to get a full understanding of their perspective about the book's plot. Were they accurate representations of what the character might feel? Were they believable? Did the recording contribute to or distract from the drama of the story? Was the background selected true to the story's setting?

_____Give students ample time to watch the Vokis of their classmates and comment on them if the online platform allows.

_____If using the free account, grab a screenshot of the Voki and link it to the Voki audio.

Extension:

Have students create Vokis to introduce units of inquiry.

Notes

#5—iPads 101

Collaborations	OVERVIEW	Troubleshooting
• Anything • Critical thinking • Decision making • Reading • Speaking/listening • Writing	Introduce iPads into a fourth grade class *Appropriate for K-6 with adaptations*	When we put iPads aside, I catch students watching something rather than listening to me. How do I control that? *Have students close the cover.*
Time Required 30 minutes, several sessions		**ISTE Standards** 1, 2, 3, 4, 6

Examples of how-to webtools for iPad training (Google for website addresses):

- *Sqooltube*
- *YouTube*

Steps

____What is an iPad? It's a brand name—not a product—for a tablet computer designed, developed and marketed by Apple and used primarily for audio-visual media such as books, games, periodicals, movies, music, and web content. It has a keyboard, but most people maneuver with finger taps and swipes.

____It does less than computers, but what it does is spectacular. Such as it's instantly on—no booting up. If you use your computer's boot-up time to take a break, that's over. It's big enough to read email, watch videos, read a book (unlike your smart phone). It isn't a camera but takes great pictures.

____What it doesn't do well is run software—MS Office, Apple software—though it can with apps.

____Every new tech appliance needs a killer app, and iPads have theirs—running apps. Thousands—tens of thousands—of them, each with a particular corner on creativity and ingenuity.

____Before handing iPads out to your students, make sure you understand what your school expects out of iPad use. Is it curriculum support or to change the way teaching is delivered? Are they to enhance pedagogy? And how will you assess the success of the iPad program? Know the expectations so there are no surprises in the end.

_____Start with an introduction to the iPad, inhand. Take a tour showing the screen (with the apps, the task bar at the bottom, the search function revealed with right swipe), the home button, the recharger (make it the student responsibility to put it back into the iPad cart plugged into the charger), the front and back camera, the microphone, the jack (for headphones—critical with 20 students in a room, all using iPads), on/off, volume, the dock.

_____Many students are familiar with iPads so start by asking them what they know about it—what's their favorite use of an iPad? As they rattle them off, share them with all students. Demonstrate and have students try them out—whether it's the camera or a tool.

_____Brainstorm for best practices in using the iPads in a classroom, proper care of the device, things students can do, but shouldn't at school. For example, don't change settings without permission, don't delete apps, don't change the wallpaper.

_____Show students how to save images to the iPad from Google, specifically for the purpose of discussing digital rights and privacy.

_____Show students how to check battery, to be sure they have enough. With a battery life approaching nine hours, that probably won't be an issue, but it's a good step to get used to.

_____Talk about how to take care of the iPad:

- *Keep it in a safe place*
- *Carry it with both hands*
- *Never run with the iPad*
- *Use it with clean hands*
- *Don't eat or drink around it*
- *Always ask permission to use*
- *Never bang on the iPad*
- *Don't delete apps or change wallpaper.*
- *Use headphones with audio*
- *Recharge at the end of the day*
- *Never purchase from the apps*

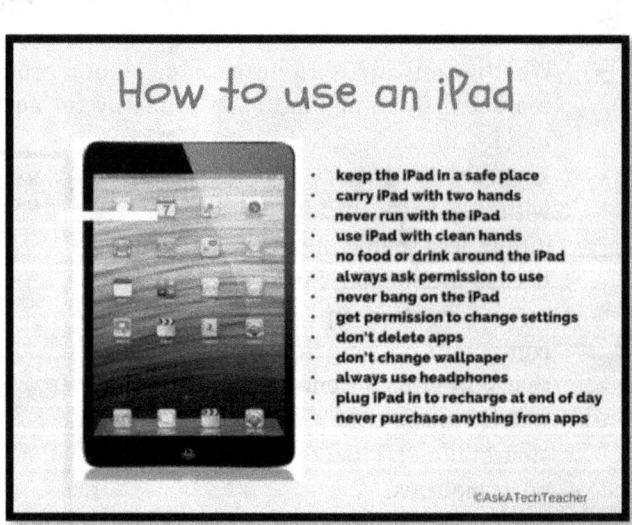

_____Create a Scavenger Hunt of the apps and functions you consider most important to students. Let them work in pairs as they explore the iPad, on a hunt for these programs. Be sure to include reading an ebook, finding their geo-location, using Google Earth, playing music (Garage Band is great), sending a note to the teacher, taking a picture of a friend, taking a picture of something on the iPad, saving a picture from the internet, finding the answer to a math problem (give them a hint as to which app would work best for that), watching a video,

_____Let students explore the apps you've installed. This will roll into a discussion of volume controls and headphones.

_____Experiment with note-taking on the iPad. Have students test out the Notes app. You may have installed another note-taking app like:

- *EverNote*
- *Google Keep*
- *Notability*
- *Note Taker HD*
- *OneNote*
- *Voice Thread*

_____Try as many apps as you can to test them. Discuss how these can cut down on paper use in the classroom.

_____Discuss the popular shortkeys:

- *Add a period*
- *Toggle between last two used apps*
- *Close current app*
- *Put something in quotation marks*
- *Break keyboard apart for easier typing*
- *Undo what was last typed*
- *Search*
- *Close all apps*

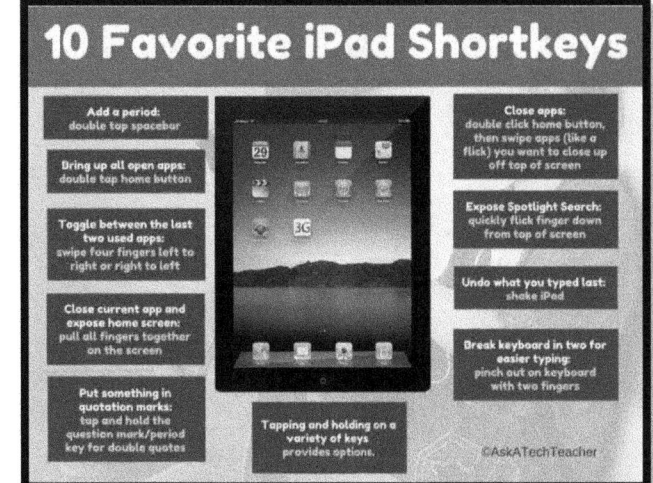

_____As a hands-on activity, have students work in groups or individually to research a topic related to a class unit (quickly). Collect all notes, images, websites through your notetaking app-of-choice. At the end, discuss how it went with the students. What are the pros and cons of using the iPad compared to paper-and-pencil? Were there any functions they couldn't do with the iPad? If so, ask for student feedback—did anyone solve that issue?

_____If you have arranged a method of accessing student network folders from the iPads, have students store all their material on the server before giving up the iPad for the day.

_____Before ending the class, have students access a poll or survey you've developed. Ask students their feedback on iPads. Include questions that assess ease of use, learning levels, engagement, educational value to students, student-centered-ness, and whatever else is important to your program. Students will love answering the questions and you'll get amazing feedback.

_____At the end of each class, establish a procedure for 'shutting down' the iPads—similar to what students do to take care of their computer station. Include wiping the screen, powering off, plugging into the cart.

Fifth Grade

#1—Scratch for Fifth Graders

Collaborations	OVERVIEW	Troubleshooting
• Anything • Critical thinking • Decision making • Literature • Math	*Develop problem-solving and critical thinking skills while scaffolding comprehension of inquiry.* ***Appropriate for grades 5-8***	I want to change the background, but there's no 'background' tab. *You're probably in the sprite screen. Click the 'stage icon and the 'background' tab will appear.*

Time Required	ISTE Standards
40 minutes (up to 6 sessions	2, 4

Here's where to find Scratch how-to instructions: For more, visit Ask a Tech Teacher coding resources:

- *MIT*
- *Scratch Ed*
- *TeacherTube*

Steps

_____ An important skill for future Middle School students is problem solving, to logically think through a situation and come up with the steps to a solution.

_____ Scratch, a free program developed and distributed by MIT, is a user-friendly introduction to programming designed to teach students logical and higher order thinking skills in a fun, motivating, and captivating way. Scratch is easy to learn, enabling students to absorb critical thinking skills while they create. Programmers know that users learn computer programming best when they can fiddle with it. The same is true with lots of problems. If the scenario is interesting enough to capture and maintain a student's attention, s/he tinkers—tries a variety of solutions, thinks through what went right and wrong and tweaks the solution until s/he gets it right. This approach personalizes learning and solution creation while it promotes the use of the iterative thinking process.

_____ Whether you're a Common Core school or not, these eight constructs from Standards for Mathematical Practice regarding critical thinking tie into Scratch programming:

- *Make sense of problems and persevere in solving them—Students must understand where they made a programming error and fix it.*
- *Reason abstractly and quantitatively—Visualizing coding requires an abstract understanding of what is occurring.*

- *Construct viable arguments and critique the reasoning of others—Coding and remixing requires students critique others' work.*
- *Model with mathematics—Translate available scripts to student needs, not unlike decoding a formula in mathematics.*
- *Use appropriate tools strategically—Coding offers a plethora of tools. The trick is to adapt strategically to student needs.*
- *Attend to precision—To get scripts to do what students want requires precision*
- *Look for and make use of structure—look at available tools, scripts, blocks, options, in selecting those which facilitate student needs*
- *Look for and express regularity in repeated reasoning—notice when a formula/program/script accomplishes goals.*

_____Provide a quick overview. Encourage students to listen for the following:

- *How do you edit background?*
- *What is broadcasting?*
- *How does one build/edit a sprite?*
- *How do you make it glide?*
- *How do you add dialogue, recordings?*
- *How do you automate movement?*
- *How do you wait (under control)?*
- *How does a sprite move forward/backward and/or flip?*

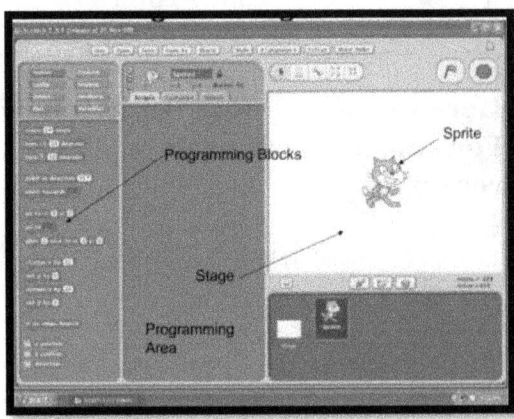

_____Open Scratch on class screen. Point out:

- *toolbars*
- *small stage, full stage, presentation mode tools*
- *how to connect and activate scripts*
- *three ways to create a Sprite and add costumes*
- *blocks—scripts that change with options*
- *control options and green flag to automate scripts*
- *programming categories (motion, looks, sound)—demonstrate each*
- *drop-down menus available on some blocks/scripts*
- *tabs for sprites/backgrounds that change depending upon which you're in*

_____Take questions but remember: You aren't teaching. You're introducing. Students are explorers and risk-takers in this project.

_____Provide a list of resources to help students find answers without asking you for help (see options at the top of this lesson).

_____Before you help, expect students to try to solve their own problem. Here are strategies they can try:

- *check resource list*
- *check Scratch website Task cards*
- *right-click on a tool and select 'help'*
- *check with a neighbor*
- *check Help (with Scratch's website)*

_____Students can work individually or in groups. Give them time to view resource list and Task cards (on the Scratch website), experiment with tools, explore functions.

_____When students have practiced skills, download a 5th grade project from the Scratch website. Find a topic similar to one they will create. Explore how this student accomplished tasks; remix to suit project needs, then save remix to student portfolio

_____Next: Students create a project aligned with class inquiry. It could support a history lesson or review a book they're reading. Give them much freedom to do in a way that works for their learning style. The insets are examples.

_____When project is completed, reflect on the Scratch experience:

- *What did student like/dislike?*
- *Was it as easy/hard as student thought it would be?*
- *What problem-solving skills did student use/learn?*
- *What other school projects could Scratch be used for?*

_____Here's a summative assessment (zoom in if necessary):

Category	Beginning	Developing	Proficient	Exceptional
Content area concepts *(Add specific targets as needed)*	__ Does not include ideas about the subject area or ideas are incorrect	__ Includes a few ideas about the subject, shows some understanding	__ Focuses on and understands important concepts about the subject matter	__ Makes important connections between subject area concepts, shows in-depth understanding
Project design	__ Did not try to make own artwork __ No clear purpose of project or organization __ Does not provide a way for other people to interact with program	__ Project uses artwork of others with some effort to change __ Has some sense of purpose and structure __ Includes way for user to interact with program, may need to be clearer or fit program's purpose better	__ Project uses original artwork or reuses imported images creatively __ Has clear purpose, makes sense, has structure __ Includes way for user to interact with program and clear instructions	__ Project artwork and creativity significantly support the content __ Has multiple layers or complex design __ User interface fits content well, is complex; instructions are well-written and integrated into design
Programming	__ Project shows little understanding of blocks and how they work together __ Lacks organization and logic __ Has several bugs	__ Project shows some understanding of blocks and how they work together __ Has some organization and logic __ May have a couple bugs	__ Project shows understanding of blocks and how they work together to meet a goal __ Is organized, logical, and debugged	__ Project shows advanced understanding of blocks and procedures __ Uses additional programming techniques __ Is particularly well organized, logical, and debugged
Process	__ Student did not get involved in design process __ Did not use project time well and did not meet deadlines __ Did not collaborate	__ Student tried out the design process __ Used project time well sometimes and met some deadlines __ Collaborated at times	__ Student used design process (stated problem, came up with ideas, chose solution, built and tested, presented results) __ Used project time constructively, met deadlines __ Collaborated appropriately	__ Student made significant use of the design process __ Used project time constructively, finished early or added additional elements __ Found ways to collaborate beyond class structure

Extension:

Have students explore the Scratch projects online and teach themselves a skill not covered in the task cards. Then, teach it to others in the class.

Write up the Scratch project in student blogs, if they have them. Comment on the posts of classmates.

If teaching youngers (K-2), try Scratch Jr.

8th Grade Technology Curriculum: Teacher Manual

#2—Digital Citizens and Internet Safety

Collaborations	OVERVIEW	Troubleshooting
• Critical thinking • Problem solving • Research • Speaking/listening	How do fifth graders work safely in a digital world they don't wholly understand?	My Admin is restrictive of Internet usage. *We can't hide students from the internet. Experts say it's better to teach them to thrive.*
Time Required 30 minutes (up to six sessions)		**ISTE Standards** 5

Examples of Digital Citizenship webtools. If you can't find these by Googling the website, visit Ask a Tech Teacher and the Digital Citizenship—Internet Safety resource page:

- *Hector's World Internet safety videos*
- *Internet safety quiz*
- *Internet Safety Tips for Parents — with a video*
- *Internet safety video–day in digcit's life*
- *NetSafety–videos on internet safety; varied age groups*
- *Safe tech use–video*

Steps

_____This unit takes 5-6 weeks, broken up into segments.

_____Every year, take time to discuss how students work safely on the internet. Review last year's discussions on digital citizens. What are the responsibilities of a digital citizen? Discuss concepts of:

- *digital privacy*
- *image copyrights*
- *public domain*
- *plagiarism*
- *netiquette*
- *cyber-bullying*
- *online presence*
- *password protections*

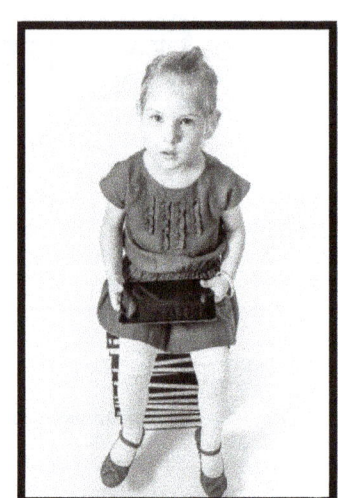

_____Solicit ideas and experiences from students.

_____Have students take the Safe Kids Quiz (Google this or find a link on the Ask a Tech Teacher Digital Citizenship resource page).

_____Go through the quiz as a class and discuss each question. Encourage students to be open and honest with their answers. Respect their thoughts and guide them as necessary.

_____What should students do if they accidently come to a 'bad' website? What do they do now? Discuss. How has what they do now changed from when they were in, say, second grade?

_____Discuss that it's difficult to tell what's true online. It's easy to lie when no one can see you or find you.

_____Show a fake picture (you can find many on the internet or by Googling 'Is This Picture Real?' Why do they think the image is true? Or not true? Why do they think so many people fell for its message?

_____Here are options (find these links and others on Ask a Tech Teacher Digital Citizenship—Internet Hoaxes resource page):

- *Fake baseball blog--well done*
- *Save the tree octopus*

_____Play the Factitious game to test student skills on telling the difference between fake and fact.

_____Try the WebQuest, *Hoax or Not?* designed to help students learn how to evaluate whether or not a website is fact or fake. Discuss it when students finish.

_____If you have time, *Checkology* is a great four-unit program to teach the differences between fake and fact. Discuss it when they're finished.

_____Introduce a discussion of **Facebook**. What is it? Who uses it? Who has friends or siblings who do? Fifth graders are too young to have Facebook accounts (the minimum age is 13) so why discuss this? Because students have siblings using it or use it illegally themselves. Discussing it with 5th graders will put you ahead of the curve on knowing how to use this site safely.

_____What does 'digital citizenship' have to do with Facebook?

_____What is the safest way to use Facebook? How do students know who the people that want to be friends are? Does anyone have experience with family members on Facebook?

_____Discuss adult attitudes about Facebook. Do students' parents understand online social media? Technology in general? How many students think they know more about technology than their parents? Does this matter when students are making decisions about the use of online media?

_____As a general rule: Don't do anything online you can't tell your parents about. Pretend they see/read/hear everything you say on Facebook.

_____Depending upon your school, you may want to Google 'facebook'+'fifth grade' and share some of the scare stories you find. Yes, even in fifth grade, they're scary.

_____What's a 'digital footprint'? Discuss this with students, with the goal a definition similar to:

a digital footprint is the amount of content, whether it be words, photographs, audio, or video, that is traceable back to a given individual. Your digital footprint includes photographs uploaded to sites like Flikr, blog posts, video files, posts you wrote on friends' Facebook Walls, and posts to your Facebook wall by your friends. Two things are most notable about the Digital Footprint 1) it can be permanent; 2) many of us search the digital footprint of peers and are influenced by what we find.

_____Explain its significance. When should students start using their proper name and photo rather than an avatar? Who is responsible for explaining how to be internet savvy? What information is included on website and blog (and social media) profiles?

_____Google yourself for students and display the results on the class screen (Do this prior to displaying it to be sure the results are appropriate for your class).

_____Have students search their name on Google (they might find more if they type their school with it). What do they think of the information posted about them? Is it accurate? Wrong?

_____Now search their parent's name. Explain how this relates to 'digital footprint' and why that's important, even in fifth grade.

Extension:

Use sponge or free time to reinforce these concepts by circling back on them constantly.

Take one of the books students are reading this year. Have each student set up a 'mock' Facebook page as though they were a character in the book. This should include the profile data, images, Likes, friends, and status updates. Post them on the class blog or website so students can comment, friend them, ask questions.

Notes

8th Grade Technology Curriculum: Teacher Manual

#3—Tessellations Around the World

Collaborations	OVERVIEW	Troubleshooting
• Art • Geology • Geometry • Math • Problem solving	*Students understand math and nature have a lot of similarities* **Appropriate for grades 3-8 with adaptations**	1) I can't line the chevrons up. *Use gridlines to help.* 2) How do I select multiple cells? *Ctrl+click on each cell.*
Time Required 30 minutes (2 sessions)		**ISTE Standards** 1, 2, 4

Examples of tessellation webtools. If you can't find these by Googling the website, visit Ask a Tech Teacher Math resource page:

- *National Library of Virtual Manipulatives*
- *Tessellations and Escher*

Steps

____A tessellation is a puzzle that repeats a particular pattern like a honeycomb. It helps students 1) understand geometric principles as they experiment with shapes, and 2) identify patterns, a critical piece of problem solving.

____Discuss M. Escher and his paintings with tessellations. Maybe the art class does these drawings—check and connect if possible.

____Note the common occurrences of tessellations in nature and elsewhere (i.e., mudflats, a sunflower, a giraffe, and a honeycomb). Discuss their mathematical pattern. When tessellations 'grow up', they're called fractals.

____Ask students to identify tessellations they find in their lives (scales on a fish, a tortoise shell, a pineapple), in class (the Blue Mosque and the Hagia Sophia use tessellating patterns in their designs), and in the classroom. Here are examples:

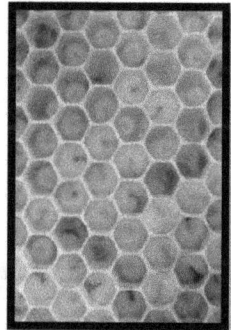

_____Show tessellations on the class screen. Have students determine the characteristics associated with tessellations (i.e. repeating patterns, no overlapping, no gaps).

_____Have students create a simple tessellation in a spreadsheet (i.e., Excel or Sheets). Use only one shape.

_____Open Excel. By fifth grade, students are probably familiar with a spreadsheet program so ask one of the students to provide an overview of rows, columns, toolbars, canvas, and whatever else seems important to them.

_____Select 'autoshapes. Then select the 'chevron' autoshape and paint it onto the spreadsheet. Make it two rows tall and three columns wide. Copy-paste it multiple times.

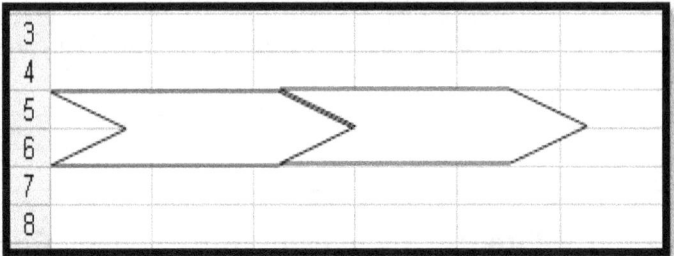

_____Arrange the shapes nose to nose. Use gridlines to be sure they're aligned,

_____Use the paint bucket to color the shapes in a pattern.

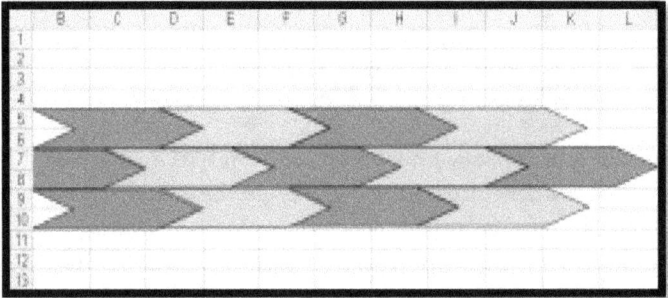

Extension:

Try other autoshapes. Which ones work and which don't. Why?

Upload a tessellation found around the school to a program like Voki. Record audio notes over the picture and share with friends.

Try NLVM's virtual manipulatives--tessellations.

Discuss the use of tessellations in optical illusions. See examples below:

#4—Google Earth Literary Tour

Collaborations	OVERVIEW	Troubleshooting
• Geography • Literature • Writing	*Students create a Google Earth tour about a book read in class* ***Appropriate for grades 4-8***	My tour disappeared *Back up tours every class. Class computers are used by many students who might mistakenly delete work.*
Time Required 30 minutes (6 sessions)		**ISTE Standards** 1, 2, 6

Steps

____Google Earth is a popular program with students. It never fails to garner their interest, full attention, and commitment to the project.

____Have a student familiar with Google Earth volunteer to review the toolbars, 'My Places', 3D layer, and how to move around the globe. Have another student explain how to add a location to 'Places' and activate latitude-longitude (lat-long—the domain-specific word) grid lines, find a location, edit the dialogue box, zoom in and out, and activate 3D Buildings and Street View. Discuss uses of lats and longs. Zoom in to investigate exact locations of several landmarks. Have another student show how to measure distance.

____Show several Google Earth tours created by students last year (or use the installed one that comes with the download) to remind students how tours work.

____Notice:

1) tour locations are stored in one file folder
2) tour goes in the sequence locations are placed in file folder
3) toolbar allows students to stop the tour and zoom in for a closer look
4) students can go directly to a specific tour location

____Ask students to share practical strategies for using use Google Earth based on prior experience (by fifth grade, many students have used it for several years). If there are questions, see if classmates can answer them before providing the answer.

____This project will ask students to create a geographic tour of locations and events from a book they are reading. Discuss the book being read in class. Review setting locations, how characters are affected by them, how the author makes each location come alive with his technique and descriptive details.

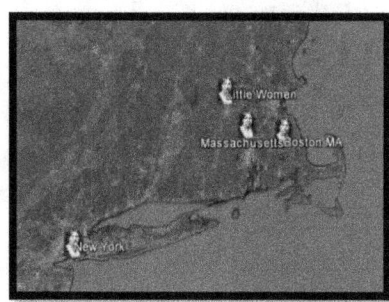

____Students will use Google Earth to place themselves in situ with the characters—see what they see, walk the streets they walk with Street View, study the buildings around them with the 3D layer—gain a rich understanding of the world they live in. For examples, Google 'Google Lit Trips'.

_____ Work in pairs. Make a file folder under 'Places' with a unique group name. This is where all locations will be saved, in the order they are visited in the story.

_____ Find the geographic location where the book starts. Use 3D and Street view to explore. Create a customized placemark (a character or student picture to mark all locations on student tour) and label it with the book title. Provide a synopsis in placemark dialogue.

_____ Add five-ten placemarks to mark high points, events, significant locations. Tell the story by writing notes in the placemark dialogue box. Include:

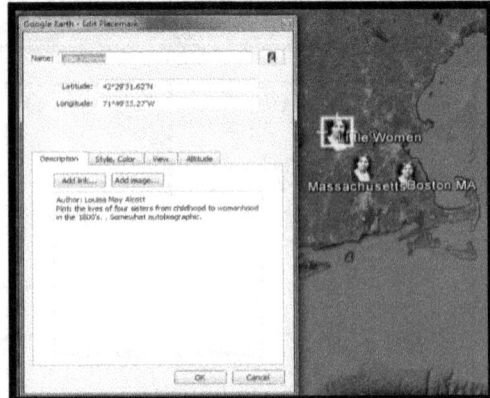

- *a plot summary based on geographic location*
- *a character introduction based on where they live or places they go during the story*
- *quotes from the book with citations*
- *academic words student didn't know and their meaning (defined by story context)*
- *key concepts about important characters, plot points, settings*
- *insight into effect of geography on story*
- *relevant facts, definitions, concrete details, quotations, examples*
- *other information on characters, plot, setting, story arc to summarize story*

_____ Save all placemarks to the student 'My Tour' folder in the correct order. Show students how to copy-paste bookmarks from 'temp' folder and drag-drop locations to re-order their appearance in the tour.

_____ Each class period, back up folder to student digital portfolio. This is critical because most school digital devices are used by multiple students.

_____ By end of the tour, viewers should have a solid overview of book, characters, setting, plot, events, and how geography impacted the progression of the story.

_____ At least three placemarks must include images as well as dialogue. Use 'add image' button in placemark dialogue box. URLs of images can be found on the internet or from one you've uploaded to a photo sharing website.

_____ If using the internet, remind students how to do so safely and as good digital citizens.

_____ At least three placemarks must include links to resource sites that support events in book. This will allow interested readers to dig deeper as their curiosity is piqued.

_____ Add one image overlay to represent characters in story.
_____ Measure distance between locations using Google Earth ruler. This data should be relevant to the story and included in placemark dialogue (for example, *how far did a character travel to get to scene of the crime?*).
_____ When the student thinks they are done, review with a neighbor using the rubric. Are all elements included? Is tour clear? Does neighbor understand story? Does tour run well? Plan, revise, edit, and rewrite as needed.

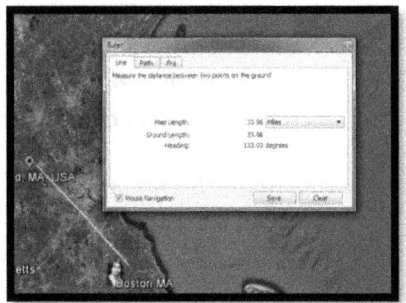

Google Earth Tour
Grading Rubric

Your name: _____

Teacher: _____

GE Tour — 1 points
- Folder w/ student name
- Tour runs

Sufficient Placemarks — 15 points
- 5-15 geographic locations
- Locations include fact

Each Placemark... — 3 points
- Placed geographically
- Labeled correctly
- Placemark customized

Professional Look — 1 points

_____ Optional: Record tour using GE's 'Record a Tour' tool. Save to student digital file or save /publish/share as is the custom in your school.
_____ Save image of Lit Tour to the student digital portfolio and/or embed tour with a reflection to student blog, website, or wiki. Discuss how geography was critical to story events and how Google Earth provided the right canvas for sharing ideas. How did this digital tool enable a better/stronger/more relevant discussion on issues than word processing or slideshows? Thoughts should be objective, on-point, with precise and domain-specific language appropriate to the task, audience, and purpose.

Extension:

Create a tour based on history being studied, i.e., Worldwide Civil Wars.

Create a Google Earth tour of an Immigrant's travels to the Colonies that shows an English immigrants' path from England to the colonies. Personalize the placemark so it pictures the immigrant selected (i.e., a young lass from Ireland's countryside). Mark the location where they started and in the discussion box, share why they are leaving the life they know for one they don't. Mark their first stop in America and share their feelings, emotions, first experiences in the New World. Mark each location as they make their journey, creating a new life for themselves.

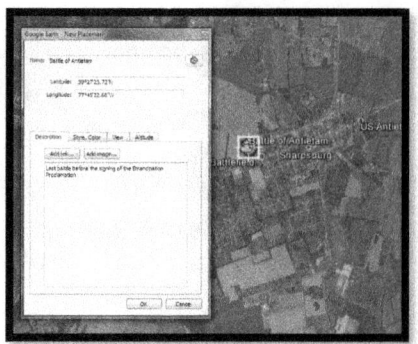

Have students present their tour to the class. Encourage them to dress in costume to create an overall effect.

Instead of Google Earth use, Google Maps or Google Tour Builder

Notes

Sixth Grade

#1—Digital Citizenship 101

Collaborations	OVERVIEW	Troubleshooting
• Art • Digital citizenship • Researching • Writing	Review and expand on digital citizenship. *Appropriate for grades 6-8*	*I can't find the copyright. If you can't find it, don't' use it—that's a rule of thumb for the legal use of copyrights.*
Time Required 30 minutes (6 sessions)		**ISTE Standards** 5

Examples of Digital Citizenshipship webtools. If you can't find these on Google, visit Ask a Tech Teacher and the Digital Citizenship—Copyright Law resource page:

- *Copyright and Fair Use*
- *Copyright Basics (Washburn University)*
- *What is Digital Law (a video)*
- *A Fair(y) Use Tale (video)*
- *Copyright Explained (fun video, informative)*
- *Wanna Work Together (Creative Commons)*
- *Copyright curriculum (Teaching Copyright.org)*
- *Take the mystery out of copyrights–Library of Congress*

Steps

____This unit takes 5-6 weeks. Every year, discuss how students stay safe on the internet.

____Review last year's discussions on digital citizens. Discuss concepts of:

- digital privacy
- difficulty of telling what's true online
- image copyrights, public domain
- plagiarism
- online presence
- password protections
- Facebook and other social media
- netiquette
- digital footprints and the importance of having a positive digital footprint

> The law states that works of art created in the U.S. after January 1, 1978, are automatically protected by copyright once they are fixed in a tangible medium (like the internet) BUT a single copy may be used for scholarly research (even if that's a 2nd grade life cycle report) or in teaching or preparation to teach a class.

____Solicit ideas and experiences from students.

____Digitally delivered content is everywhere but few understand the legalities of usage and sharing. It's not uncommon that parents and fellow teachers don't follow legal steps when using online material, thus providing inaccurate role models for students. How many of you have seen colleagues provide a linkback to an image and think that's all they need do to comply with legal requirements?

_____When I teach professional development classes, by far the topic that surprises teachers the most is the legal use of online images. And they're not alone. On my blog, in educator forums, and in the virtual meetings I moderate, there's lots of confusion about what can be grabbed for free from online sites and what must be cited with a linkback, credit, author's name, public domain reference, or even as involved as an email from the creator giving you permission. When I receive guest posts that include pictures, many contributors tell me the photo can be used because they include the linkback.

_____Not always true. In fact, the answer to the question...

"What online images can I use?"

typically starts with...

It depends...

_____Here's the basic law as it applies to the US (simplified—see inset at the start of this lesson):

> *The law states that works of art created in the U.S. after January 1, 1978 are automatically protected by copyright once they are fixed in a tangible medium (like the internet) BUT a single copy may be used for scholarly research (even if that's a 2nd grade life cycle report) or in teaching or preparation to teach a class.*

_____This explains the bare bones of copyright as well as the 'Fair Use' exclusion that allows teachers and students to use copyrighted materials one time for educational purposes.

_____For an overview of copyrighting, watch the video *'Copyright Explained'* (you can find that link in Ask a Tech Teacher's resource pages).

_____Broadly defined, here are four ways to copyright images:

- *Legal copyright*
- *Fair Use*
- *Creative Commons*
- *Public Domain*

Legal copyright

_____This is when a person holds the legal right to all distribution and use of the media. In the absence of any other permissions, you can't use these materials without getting the approval from the creator

Fair Use

_____While laws surrounding 'fair use' are more involved than what I'll discuss here, for education purposes, American copyright law provides the legal use of one copy of media for the purposes of education. That covers you if you're the teacher or student but only for educational purposes. This may or may not apply to other nations so be cautious when the image you'd like to use is from a non-American website.

Creative Commons

_____This is a popular and accepted way to parse copyrights that creators wish to have attached to their work. This can be anything from no copyright to only use by following the guidelines provided by the creator. The (free) license you sign up for includes icons that indicate the level of copyright.

Public Domain

_____The creator retains no rights. Users can use the creation for any purpose with no attribution, linkback, credit, or citation.

_____To find the copyright of an image or other media, check the website for 'Privacy' or 'Terms of Use'. Below is an example of where copyrights are found in a few images:

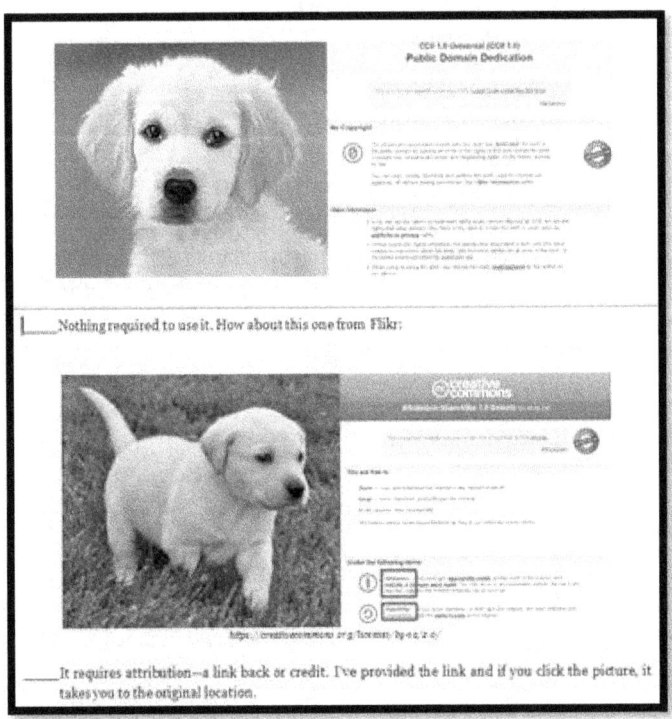

_____Nothing required to use it. How about this one from Flikr:

_____It requires attribution—a link back or credit. I've provided the link and if you click the picture, it takes you to the original location.

____The only safe images are 1) those you created, and 2) most images that are 70 years older than the death of the creator. Others are subject to the rules of the creator. Even 'Public Domain' isn't always safe because some are misfiled.

____How would you feel if someone stole your artwork (or music, videos, or text) and posted it online? What if they made ugly comments about it? What if they made money off it?

____It happens all the time, sometimes maliciously and other times because the people doing it don't know any better. Let's talk about how to fix that lack of knowledge.

- *First: To prevent it happening to you, add a copyright notice announcing that all media contained on your website is protected by copyright laws and cannot be used without permission.*
- *Second: Make it habit to NOT use images not freely available.*
- *Third: Occasionally, grab one of your personal creative artworks (drawings, photos, or other images) and drop it into either Images.google.com or Tineye.com to see where it has been used online.*
- *Last: Never assume an image is free to use. If you can't find the copyright notice, pick a different image. But, you say, tracking down the source of an image and finding the copyright language is difficult. Yes, and necessary.*

Notes

#2—Twitter in Education

Collaborations	OVERVIEW	Troubleshooting
• Communication • Critical thinking • Reading • Socializing • Writing	*Teach concise, pithy writing with Twitter's 280-character limit* ***Appropriate for grades 6-8 with adaptations***	Parents object to social media in class. *Talk with them before using it. Discuss their concerns. Explain why it is a good idea. Same goes for your Admin—they may also need convincing.*
Time Required 45 minute intro, 5-10 minutes, repeat		**ISTE Standards** 2, 4, 5

Steps

_____ For anyone who missed it, Twitter switched its app category from 'social media' to 'news'. It makes sense; tweets and twitter streams have been part of hard-core news reports for years as an effective way for leaders and politicians to reach their constituents and pollsters to gauge what interests people.

_____ Twitter's gossipy reputation among administrators and most parents negates its dynamic applications in the classroom. Educators can use it as a student-friendly approach to everything from assessment to sharing notes.

_____ Before unpacking Twitter in your class, here are guidelines:

- *Clear its use with your administration. Be prepared to educate them on why what seems to be social media is actually educational.*
- *Inform parents that their children will use Twitter to collaborate, share information, and study. Be prepared to explain the benefits of a Twitter-powered class.*
- *Twitter doesn't have a lower age limit but does reference 'thirteen' as a suggested minimum age. You decide what fits your group. You may also decide that setting the Twitter stream as private (called 'protected Tweets') is a good educational decision or having a class Twitter feed that you monitor is appropriate.*

- *Demonstrate how to use Twitter and what the symbols mean (tie this into a class discussion on math symbols).*
- *Establish rules for Twitter use. Remind students it is for education, not chatting and socializing. Then enforce it by suspending privileges, warning abusers, or whatever works best in your class climate.*
- *Check out the Twitter streams of other educators.*

_____Some of the most common reasons teachers like Twitter include:

- *To stay in touch with parents*
- *To stay in touch with (older) students*
- *For last-minute updates on projects, classwork*

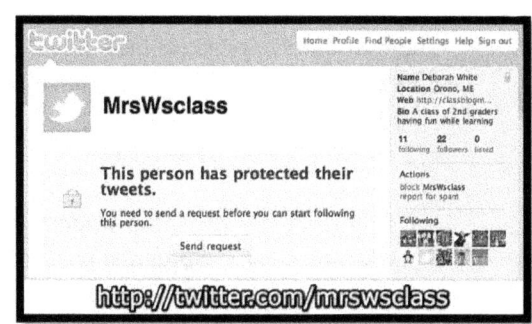

_____These make sense. MS—or HS--students are more likely to be online than at the library. Why not reach them where they 'live'?

_____Let's back up. Do you want to encourage the use of Twitter? Research says, *Yes*. From Twitter, students learn:

- **Manners**--Social networks are about netiquette. People thank others for assistance, ask politely for help, encourage contributions from others. Use this framework to teach students how to engage in a community–be it physical or virtual.
- **To be focused**--With only 280 characters, you can't get off topic or cover tangential ideas. State your main topic and your thoughts, not your meanderings. When you force yourself to write this way, you find it really doesn't take a paragraph to make a point. Use the right words, people get it. Consider that the average reader gives a story seven seconds before moving on.
- **To share**--Maybe the class is studying Ancient Greece. Have each student share their favorite website (using a #hashtag — maybe #ancientgreece) to the class Twitter stream and create a resource others can use.
- **The art of "headlining"**--Writers call this the title. Bloggers call it the headline. It must be cogent and pithy enough to pull the audience in and make them read the article. That's a tweet.
- **Conversation**--Yes. This is the world of social networks where people will read what you say and comment. It's feedback and builds an online community, be it for socializing or school. Students learn to construct their arguments expecting others to respond, question, comment. Not only does this develop the skill of persuasive writing, students learn to have a thick skin, take comments with a grain of salt and two grains of aspirin.

- **Tolerance for all opinions**--Why? Because Tweeple aren't afraid to voice their thoughts. Because the Twitter stream is a public forum (in a classroom, the stream can be private, but still visible to all members of the class), students understand what they say is out there forever. Take the opportunity to teach students about their public profile. Represent themselves well with good grammar, good spelling, well-chosen tolerant ideas. Don't be emotional or spiteful because it can't be taken back. Rather than shying away from exposing students to the world at large, use Twitter to teach students how to live in it.

_____For this grade level (6th grade, lower, and even most of MS), set up a Twitter account for your class. Make it private so no one can follow or view tweets without being a member. If students are thirteen or older, each student can also have to have a personal Twitter account. Have them set those up and 'follow' the class account.

_____Explain how Twitter works.

_____Explain ground rules: 1) use good grammar and spelling, 2) tweets are G rated and school-specific

Extension:

There are lots of projects that include Twitter in inquiry. Here are a few that you might like to try. Pick one (or more) that suits your class environment:

- **Answer tech problems**

Create a class #hashtag students use to ask for tech help (like #QesadoTech). Students post their question and answer those of classmates. It's a crowdsourced Twitter-powered helpline that will save time and answer most issues. Don't jump in to help until you're sure no one else can.

- **Backchannel device**

As you present the lesson, students provide feedback by using Twitter as a backchannel. Using a pre-agreed #hashtag, they weigh in on confusing parts or questions they have without disrupting the flow of the class. The #hashtag Twitter stream is displayed on the class screen where students can answer each other's questions or add their thoughts. You can even embed that stream with a widget provided by Twitter. Yes, it takes management and some practice, but provides a durable resource to be used for review and study.

- **Formative assessment**

Ask a summative question about the lesson and have students answer via Twitter (with the unique #hashtag). The question should be brief, within the limitations of 280 characters. As answers arrive, you'll get a good overview of student understanding on a topic. This can be live-streamed to the class screen or kept private. You can also tweet out a short on-topic video or image and ask for student reactions.

- **Group study session**

Students join a Twitter Chat to review material or complete a group project. This can happen from anywhere, any time, from most digital devices. No driving required; no central location; no dress code.

- **Notetaking**

Students take notes using a pre-arranged #hashtag.

- **Twitter novel**

If you search #twitternovel, you'll find amazing examples, dating back half a decade.

#3—Formulas in Spreadsheets

Collaborations	OVERVIEW	Troubleshooting
• Information fluency • Math • Research • Statistics	Use the excitement of formulas to support math concepts. **Appropriate for grades 6-8**	The formulas don't make sense. Visit the Ask a Tech Teacher Video resource page or Math-Videos resource page

Time Required	ISTE Standards
40 minutes (3 sessions)	3, 6

Steps

____Discuss what students remember about spreadsheets from prior years. Where have they used them? What is a spreadsheet? Name some spreadsheet programs. Why is it important to be able to use them? Prod students for answers that include:

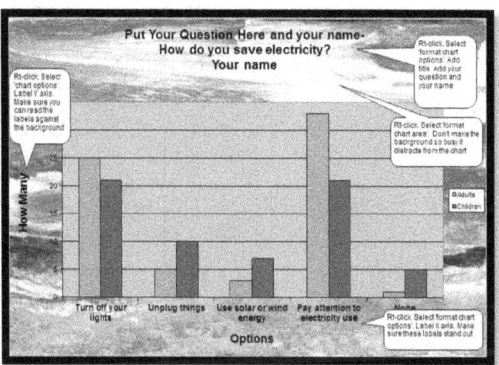

- *communicate information and ideas effectively*
- *present relationships clearly and efficiently (from Common Core)*
- *develop a coherent understanding of a topic or issue (from Common Core)*

____Discuss how spreadsheets are uniquely qualified to assist in the following (from Common Core):

- *Make sense of problems and persevere in solving them (charts/graphs)*
- *Reason abstractly and quantitatively (sorting is pivotal to spreadsheets*

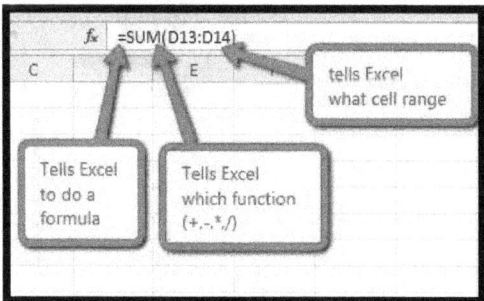

- *Use appropriate tools strategically (spreadsheet is the right tool to share data)*

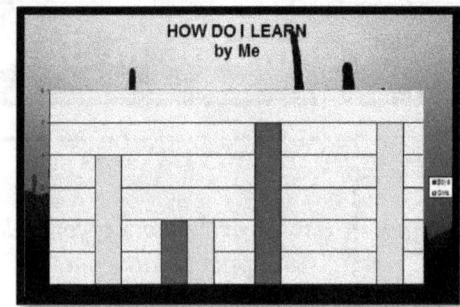

- *Construct viable arguments and critique reasoning of others (quantifiable arguments are defensible and convincing)*

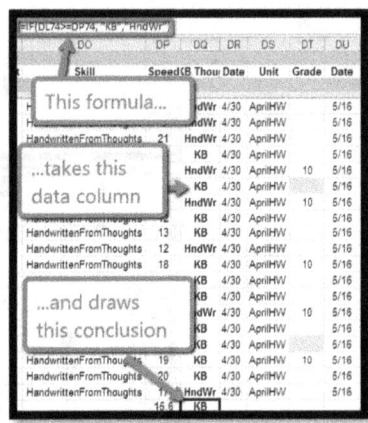 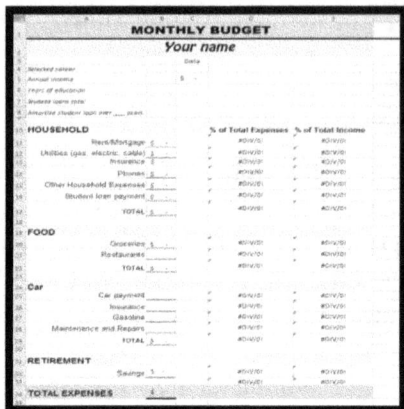

- *Model with mathematics (i.e., a monthly budget)*
- *Attend to precision (with a spreadsheet's mathematical properties*

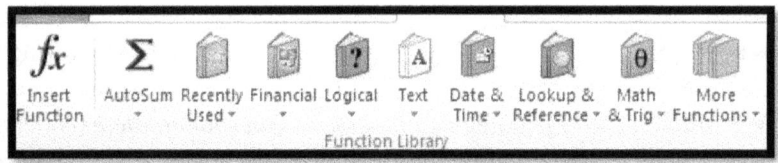

- *Look for and make use of structure (formulas, charts, graphs)*

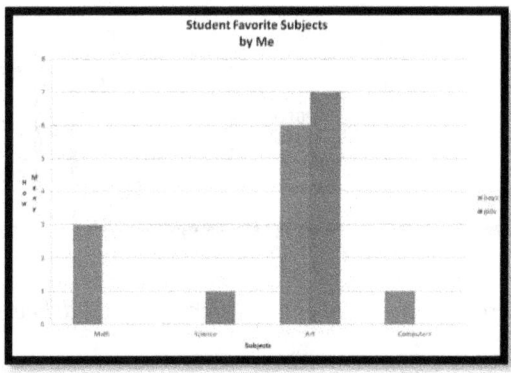

8th Grade Technology Curriculum: Teacher Manual

_____Have a student review the class spreadsheet program (Excel or Sheets)--screen, tools, tabs, ribbons. How similar they are to Word and Publisher. Review the basics—rows, columns, cells, naming protocol for cells, worksheets, workbooks. If no students feel comfortable doing this, you can review.

_____What tasks are better suited to spreadsheets than word processing? Slideshows? DTP? Here's a chart itemizing the critical elements of slideshows, word processing, spreadsheets, and desktop publishing program. Evaluate how to decide which is best suited to particular task-audience-purpose:

Element	Presentation	Word processing	Spread-- sheets	DTP
Purpose	Share a presentation	Share words	Turn numbers into information	Share information using a variety of media
Basics	Graphics-based. Design is important to content. Layout communicates. Few words, lots of images	Text-based. Design is secondary to content. Layout may detract from words. Primarily words communicate	Number-based. Focus on tables, graphs. Little text; lots of statistics and date. Almost no words	Mix of media—equal emphasis on text, images, layout, color
Sentences	Bulleted, phrases	Full sentences with proper conventions	None	Full sentences, bullets,
Content	Slides cover basics, to remind presenter what to say	Thorough discussion of a topic. Meant to be complete document	Statistics, data, charts, graphs	To draw an audience in;
Use	As a back-up to presentation	As complete resource	To support other presentation methods	Good way to group information for easy consumption
Presentation	Speaker presents with their back to the slideshow	Speaker reads from document	Speakers uses it in a presentation or 1:1	Speaker passes out as a handout or take-way
What else				

_____Open the class spreadsheet program (Excel, Spreadsheets, Numbers, or another).
_____This lesson includes two projects:

- *basic data collection*
- *create a gradebook*

Basic data collection

_____**Option 1:** Collect data from whatever source you prefer. It might be from a speed quiz taken in class (as in the inset) or something else. This can be as thorough or simple as you like.

_____Name the worksheet. Label one column for each piece of data to be collected. For example, WPM and Grade.

_____Add data collection cells such as in the inset for 'average', 'count', 'max', and 'min'.

_____Once students have recorded all information, have them evaluate the results to find average, median, and whatever else is pertinent to your class.

_____**Option 2:** Play a game using the spreadsheet to track data. You might use Coolmath's Coffee Shop and Lemonade Stand (Google 'coolmath games'). You might also use a program like PNC's Gift Hunt or Christmas Price Index.

T2 SPEED QUIZ		
	WPM	Grade
1	22	9
2	21	10
3	19	6
4	14	8
5	21	8
6	24	8
7	29	10
8	28	10
9	19	9
10	21	10
11	15	8
12	17	10
13	16	10
14	19	10
15	20	10
16	18	10
17	14	10
18	20	10
average	19.83333	9.222222
count	18	18
max	29	10
min	14	6

Create a grading sheet

_____Students create a grading sheet with formulas that automatically update class grades. It might look like the inset below with the columns required to track the student's grades and projects. Leave room for formulas that find the *Total* score and the *Average*.
_____Students can format to suit their needs (fonts, colors, sizes, fills, classes, borders). All formulas must work.
_____If necessary, provide a list of how-to videos easily found on YouTube.

	A	B	C	D	E	F	G	H	I	J	K	L	M	N	O	P	Q	R	S
1							Gradebook												
2							Your Name												
3																			
4		Extra credit	Lost points	Joined Class Discussion	Prepared for class	Problem-solving	Used tech knowledge	Updated Portfolio	Class Presenta	Project #1	Project #1	Project #1	Project #1	Project #1	Project #1	Project #1	Project #1	Total	Average
5	Class #1																		
6	Class #2																		
7	Class #3																		
8	Class #4																		
9																			
10																			

_____You may watch one video as a group and then ask students: *What should be changed to adapt the video instructions to class's needs?*
_____When the gradebook layout is complete, students add their grades and watch it calculate the summative grade.
_____What if a grade is weighted? Toss this around with students. How would they create a formula to weight the grade?
_____Have students submit their updated spreadsheet weekly.

Notes

_____
_____
_____
_____
_____
_____
_____
_____

#4—Keyboarding: Touch Typing

Collaborations	OVERVIEW	Troubleshooting
• Reading • Speaking/listening • Writing	*Develop touch typing skills.* *Appropriate for grades 6-8*	I can't type with hands covered. *Keep practicing*

Time Required	ISTE Standards
15 minutes, repeat	6

Examples of keyboarding webtools. Either Google for these or visit Ask a Tech Teacher's Keyboarding resource pages:

- *All the Right Type*
- *Goodtyping*
- *Learn2Type*
- *NitroType*
- *Peter's Online Typing*
- *Popcorn Typer*
- *TypeDojo — word lists, 10-key, and more*
- *Typing Test*

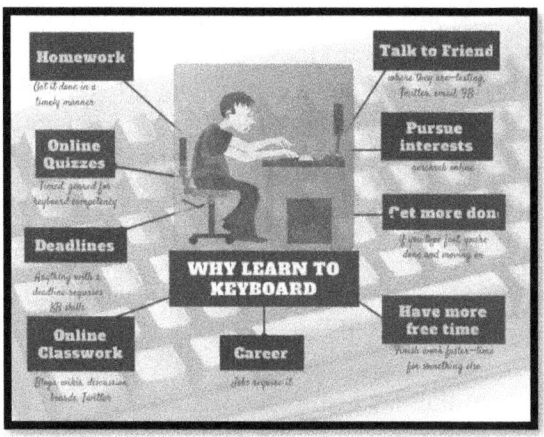

Steps

____Keyboarding is a cumulative skill – what can be effectively learned in sixth grade depends heavily upon what has been learned in prior years. It's important that students concentrate on skills like body position, hand position, and key placement.
____Basics to focus on:

- Use correct posture at the computer
    - *Keep elbows close to your sides*
    - *Keep fingers slightly curved*
    - *Sit straight, centered in front of keyboard, feet flat*
- Key with a steady even pace
- Touch type words with correct reaches , eyes on copy or screen—NOT keyboard
- Use enter, shift, tab, spacebar, and return with correct reaches
- Use keyboard shortcuts (i.e., Ctrl+P, Ctrl+S, Ctrl+c, Ctrl+V, Alt+tab, Shift+Alt+D)
- Apply keyboarding skills whenever possible, not just during typing practice

_____As you explain skills, demonstrate. Many students don't understand what 'reach' means or 'rhythmically'.

_____Spend two weeks on each row—home row, QWERTY row, and lower row. Practice using a program that focuses only on those rows such as Popcorn Typer, Type Dojo, Peter's Online Typing Course. Students practice during class (fifteen minutes a week) and at home (three sessions of fifteen minutes each, every week).

_____After six weeks (two on each of three rows), practice touch typing by mastering two-letter words (find a nice collection on Type Dojo). This will be difficult at first, and then fun—like a game. Help them stick with it through impossible to challenging to huzzah.

_____Have students take a 'test' before moving on to the graduated typing program they will spend the balance of the year on. Remember Brown Bear Typing—a favorite from kindergarten, first and second grades? Have a fifteen-minute contest to see who can get the highest score. Award the winner something that suits your student group.

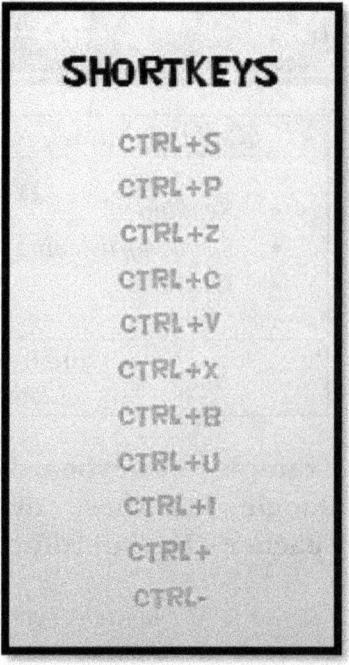

_____Now, switch to a year-long program like Type to Learn. Students spend the rest of their yearly typing practice here. Students cover hands while practicing. I provide cloths they use at school and take home if they'd like. It feels hard at first and quickly becomes easier.

_____The focus for the balance of the school year is on speed and accuracy. As students type, anecdotally observe posture, hand position, eye placement. Make suggestions when you see an endemic problem.

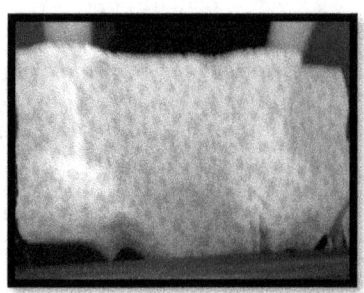

_____Each month, give a keyboard quiz to determine improvement in speed and accuracy like TypingTest.com. Have students use a different 3-minute test each time. As students take the quiz, notice who uses all fingers and correct posture.

_____The first typing quiz is the benchmark. The rest are graded based on improvement:

- 20% improvement   10/10
- 10-20% improvement   9/10
- 1-10% improvement   8/10
- No improvement   7/10
- Slowed down   6/10

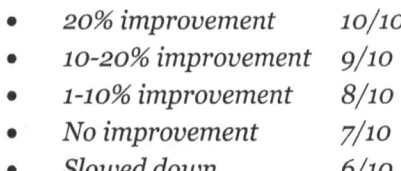

_____Grade level standards for speed and accuracy are:

5th Grade: 30 wpm
6th Grade: 35 wpm
7th Grade: 40 wpm
8th Grade: 45 wpm

_____Students who reach the grade level standard get a prize that works with your student group. Maybe, they can skip a homework.

_____Start each quarter/semester with a blank keyboard quiz. Students work in pairs to fill in key names. They must retake it until they identify all keys correctly.

_____Several times a month, do finger warm-ups. These show students that they have five working fingers, and that some are stronger than others. Remind students they have eight fingers and two thumbs—not just two pointers that hunt and peck.

Warm up Fingers

- Lay your hand flat on a table (in the inset, the book is the table) with fingers touching. Spread fingers apart as far as possible and hold for three seconds. Close fingers. Repeat 10 times.

- Next, lift each finger, move around, then lower it.

Stretch Fingers

- Hold hands facing each other. Touch thumbs. Touch first fingers, and so on. Repeat until all fingers are touching.

- With fingers pressed together, pull palms away creating a cup shape with fingers and palm. Starting at finger tips, slowly move palms closer, rolling the pressure down the fingers until fingers are pressed together. Hold for 10 seconds. Repeat 10 times.

Aerobics for Fingers

- Hold hand in the air with fingers spread like a "high-five." Move thumb to the palm and press. Bring thumb back to starting position and move the first finger to palm and press. Move it back to the starting position and repeat with remaining fingers.

  Fingers not pressing into the palm should be held straight. After one round, try again faster. Repeat 10 times, increasing speed.

Weight Training for Fingers

- Grab a scrap piece of paper and crumble it into a ball with one hand. Squeeze the paper ball tightly and hold for 10 seconds. Repeat with the other hand.

_____Keep keyboarding fun but make sure students develop good habits. They'll need these when speed and accuracy become important.

#5—Digital Posters

Collaborations	OVERVIEW	Troubleshooting
• Critical thinking • Researching • Tech concepts • Writing	Add audio, video, multi-media to the posters—and share it online *Appropriate for grades 4-8*	The digital poster has all elements but looks, well, awful. *Check design. For example, no pink font in a Glog about Ancient Greece.*
Time Required 40 minutes (2 sessions)		**ISTE Standards** 1, 2, 3, 4, 6

Examples of poster webtools. Either Google for these or visit Ask a Tech Teacher's Publishing-Posters resource pages:

- *Canva*
- *Google Draw*

Steps

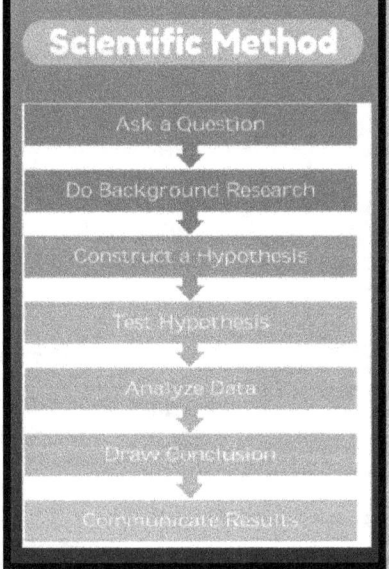

_____Posters have long been the mainstay of visual literacy—purposeful learning through a mixture of words and media. Posters are one of the most popular assessment tools. They visually display how the student communicates information and shows understanding of a topic.

_____And digital posters are the green alternative to physical posters because they accomplish the same goals without paper, driving to buy supplies, or lugging posters to school.

_____Posters can be made digitally in apps like Canva, Draw, or any number of other options. With these all-in-one program, students customize and decorate their online 'board' with text, photos, videos, graphics, sounds, drawings, data attachments and more. For example, in one of the projects, viewers can click images, visit embedded links, view the video, and even listen to original audio about *Man's trip to the Moon*.

_____Digital posters provide options to demonstrate their knowledge.

_____Open your digital poster app and demonstrate how to create one. The challenge isn't inserting pieces—images, audio, videos, text. It's getting the 'design' right—colors, animation, flow, fonts and busy-ness. Students must be sure everything meshes. Don't let a plethora of varied fonts become the message—*look what I can do with fonts*. Same with colors. All design elements must work together to convey one message, i.e., *Here's how our scientists went to the moon*. The viewer must see a seamless communication of the message without distractions.

_____Remind students that spelling and grammar—as it always does—matters, any time the written word hits a canvas. The audience that will see their work is not just the class or the school—it's the world. Create your masterpiece with that in mind.

_____Since they must access the internet to create their glogs, take this opportunity to circle back on a discussion of 'digital citizenship'. What are the best practices in creating a project viewable by the world?

_____Before starting the glog, create the 'storyboard'. What text will be included? Where will they put pictures? How about video/audio?

_____Storyboard completed, collect the pieces—images, audio, video, and text. Place everything in the student's network file folder.

_____As students work, walk around. Allow this project to be student-directed as much as possible, but where appropriate, answer questions and provide guidance.

_____When Glogs are completed, have students share them on their own wiki page or blog, and on the school blog or class website. They are easily embedded which encourages viewing by a wide audience. Once Glogs are uploaded, allow time for students to view each other's and add comments. Remind students of best practices for commenting on other's online work.

Extension:

If your school does toothpick bridges as a Middle School project, share the journey from lone toothpick to engineering feet via a Glog. Add detail about construction, the learning curve, and the result.

You as teacher might create a Glog to introduce a subject (see insert above), for example, a book students are about to read. Share images of the characters and setting. Share interesting excerpts that will peek student interest in the book. Record a summary and upload it—like the back cover on a book. Once students have seen your Glog, they'll be eager to begin reading. You can even edit the Glog as the book proceeds—add quotes the students found particularly appealing, or images that made them want to turn the pages.

Index

3D Buildings 87
ads 20, 35, 46, 106
Animoto 43, 44
Ask a Tech Teacher 15
author 17
avatars 43, 70, 73
benchmark 64
Big Huge Labs 46
blog 43, 61
book 39, 73
brainstorming 28, 29
Brown Bear Typing 32, 104
browser 54
characters 18, 73, 74
Coding 79, 80
Collaborations 14
Compare and contrast 52
copyright 43
copyright protections 17
critical thinking skills 79
cyberbullying 35, 43, 60, 68, 82
Dance Mat Typing 50, 64, 104
design 107
detail 26
digital citizen 35, 67
digital citizenship 42, 59, 67, 92, 107
Digital Commerce 70
Digital Footprint 70, 83
digital footprints 92
digital privacy 42, 45, 59, 69, 70, 82, 92
digital rights 42
digital rights and responsibilities 67, 68
digital world 34, 82
drag-and-drop 22
embed 57
Escher 85
Excel 86, 99
Facebook 70, 83, 92
fair use 70
fairy tales 28
fifth grade 33, 78
Fifth Graders 79
finger exercises 22, 30
finger warm-ups 30, 49, 65, 105
First Grade 25, 35
flip to your classroom 54
Following directions 26
formulas 99
Fourth Grade 62
Gimp 36
Google Earth 87, 89, 90
Google Earth Literary Tour 87
Google Earth tours 87
grading sheet 102
grammar 18
graphic organizers 52, 71
helpers 23, 28
historical figure 16
home row, ... 64
hunt 'n peck 48, 63
image copyrights 43, 59, 70, 82, 92
index 17
inquiry-driven 44
internet 15, 20
iPads 40, 75
keyboard shortcuts 66
Keyboarding 30, 48, 63, 103
KidPix 18, 24
Kindergarten 14, 21, 33
landforms 58
left handed 21
letters 19
library 41
math 99
Middle school 79, 97, 107
mind map 28
Model 80
mouse 21
MS Word 53
multi-media 18
netiquette 35, 42, 60, 68, 82, 93
online communications 59
online presence 43, 82, 92
password 35, 70, 92
password protections 82
photo effects 47
Photoshop 36
plagiarism 17, 18, 59, 70, 82, 92
plot items 18
plot 29
Posters 46, 106
PowerPoint 101
prefixes 18
problem solving 26, 81
public domain 70, 82, 92
puzzle 55
Puzzle Maker 54
QR code 39
QR Person 40
QWERTY 64, 104
read 17
reflect 16, 37, 40, 45, 55, 58
rubric 89
safe search methods 43
Scan 40
Scavenger Hunt 76

Scratch	79
screen shot	53
Second Grade	38
Sentences	19
setting	18, 27, 29
Shape Stroll	23
shapes	23
Sixth Grade	91
SmartArt	53
Smartscreen	17, 23, 26, 29, 57
social media	92
speed and accuracy	64, 66
spreadsheets	101
Standards for Mathematical Practice	79
stories	19
story	17
Storybird	43
storyboard	107
study guide	55
suffixes	18
Table of Contents	17
tablet computer	75
Team Challenge	66
tessellation	85
texting	69
Third Grade	33, 51
thumbnails	71
toothpick bridges	107
touch typing	63, 103
Trading Cards	47
TuxPaint	18, 24
TuxTyping	50
Type to Learn	64, 104
Type to Learn Jr.	22, 30
Typing Lessons	104
Typing Web,	50, 64
TypingTest.com	50, 66
units of inquiry	74
Venn Diagram	52
visual learners	52
Voki	70, 73
who, what, when, where, why, and how	40, 73
word processing	101
words	19
Younger Keyboarders	33

www.ingramcontent.com/pod-product-compliance
Lightning Source LLC
Chambersburg PA
CBHW080226170426
43192CB00015B/2764